YOU CAN BE
M.O.R.E.

YOU CAN BE M.O.R.E.

MOTIVATING OTHERS TO REACH EXCELLENCE

ANTHONY Q. KNOTTS

authorHOUSE®

AuthorHouse™
1663 Liberty Drive
Bloomington, IN 47403
www.authorhouse.com
Phone: 1-800-839-8640

Cover & Interior Design: LaTanya Orr,
Selah Branding and Design LLC, www.iselah.com
Editor/Proofreader: Pastor Thomas Pumphrey

Unless otherwise indicated, Scripture quotations are taken from the King James version of the Holy Bible, 1995, Zondervan Corporation, and the Holy Bible, New International Version, Copyright © 1973, 1978, 1984 by the International Bible Society. Used by permission of Zondervan Publishing House. The "NIV" and "New International Version" trademarks are registered in the United States Patent and Trademark Office by the International Bible Society.

New King James Version (NKJV) Copyright © 1979, 1980, 1982, by Thomas Nelson, Inc. Used by permission. All rights reserved. No part of this book may be reproduced in any form without permission in writing from the author.

All stories related in the book are true, however, most of the names have been changed to protect the privacy of the people mentioned.

Published by AuthorHouse   09/19/2012

ISBN: 978-1-4772-5738-8 (sc)
ISBN: 978-1-4772-5739-5 (hc)
ISBN: 978-1-4772-5740-1 (e)

Library of Congress Control Number: 2012914569

Any people depicted in stock imagery provided by Thinkstock are models, and such images are being used for illustrative purposes only.
Certain stock imagery © Thinkstock.

This book is printed on acid-free paper.

PRAISE FOR
"You Can Be M.O.R.E."

"Anthony Knotts is a powerful visionary! This book is a must read for those who want to improve their lives and take their God-given skills to another level. Anthony Knotts is a great teacher, preacher, motivator, entrepreneur, friend, and family man! If you truly want to change your future, develop hope and dreams, then You Can Be MORE is definitely for you."

—Edward L. Cobbler, President
ELC Investigative Services

"Anthony Knotts is a Pastorpreneur; a Pastor who understands Kingdom Principles to move the masses to MORE. If you desire MORE time . . . More Money or even More Freedom this book, You Can Be MORE, is not just for you but for anyone you care about. There are principles in this book that standing alone would create transformation in the lives of anyone who wants MORE."

—William V. Thompson,
Lead Financial Strategist
Dynamic Financial Training

"Pastor Knotts' book is a great read for MEN in all walks of life. He is very transparent in sharing hard times and bad decisions and how he has overcome through God's grace. The Lord is good and has put us in a profession to lead young men and we as coaches must accept the challenge to use the platform he has given us. You Can Be M.O.R.E. has already been and will continue to be useful in our walk. We highly recommend this book to read and study."

—Dan Brooks
Assistant Head Coach
Clemson University Football

In Memory of
George G. Knotts
December 11, 1973-June 8, 1998

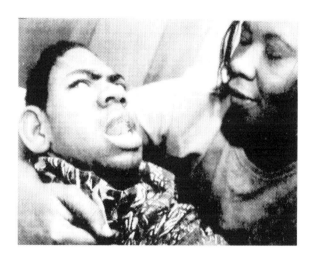

*This book is dedicated to my late brother, George,
who inspired me to be, do, and have MORE. I am thankful for
the time I was allowed to share with you and hope that
I have made you proud.*

Acknowledgments

I must thank my Lord and Savior, Jesus Christ who died so that I can be, do, and have MORE.

To my wife, First Lady Byrdzetta Knotts: Thank you for being my Abigail during my foolish periods and my Abishag, who kept my dreams, visions, and anointing warm. Words cannot express my gratitude for you being my helpmeet.

To my children, Teland, Jalen and Destiny: Thank you for the sacrifice of sharing me with the church and with the world. You are the driving force behind my desire to be, do, and have MORE.

To my Mom: Thank you for being my foundation, my pillars, and for the sacrifice you made with hard work. Most importantly, thank you for being my Hannah and giving me back to the Lord. I am what I am because of your love and support.

To my Dad: You taught me more than you'll ever know.

To my sisters, Connie and Chrissy: Thank you for being wonderful sisters.

To my staff, Tesha, Jessica, Nicole: Thank you for reading, editing, encouraging, believing, and for being midwives; Denicia, Shanika, Aundrea, Martin, Darrell: Thank you for your faithfulness.

To The Embassy: Thank you ALL, past, present and future. Most of all, thank you to those who have remained consistent during my periods of adversity. You have been my Aaron and Hur, lifting my hands when I felt weak and weary.

To Pastor Thomas Pumphrey: Thank you for using blue instead of red (inside joke).

To Jacenta Cobb: Thank you for all of your help and inspiring me to write.

To my mentors and coaches: Billy & Kay Burnett, Bert May, Larry Adkins, Tony Fortenberry, Jack Davis (J5), Larry Beck, Sandy Morris, and Charlie England (Rest in Peace).

To my teachers: Geraldine Beauford, Martha Clement (Rest in Peace), Ellen Garner, Kathy Mizenheimer, Amy Bailey, Kawana Crump, and Becky Griffin.

To Chad Griffin: Thank you for putting me on your birthday cake when you were five years old. You let me know that I could be MORE.

To Uncle Bo & Aunt Stelle, Tony Clark, and Dennis "Bird" Scott: who taught me the meaning of pushing beyond what is expected.

To Mom & Pop Hailey: Thank you for the Friday nights at your house when I was going through adversity. You showed me then that despite my circumstances, I could be MORE.

To Pastor Randy Scott, Pastor John Cade, Robert Scott, Bishop Kenneth Yelverton, Pastor R.A. Vernon, Pastor Brenda Timberlake: Thank you.

To Superintendent Herbert Davis: Man, I love you. Thanks for your stickability; Superintendent Anthony Gilyard: You are my Jonathan; Bishop Wayne Malcolm: My life coach—Thank you for your friendship, knowledge and information, and for contributing to this book, as well as to my life; Dr. Wanda A. Davis: Thanks for being my nurse when the demons from hell were trying to destroy me and for writing a phenomenal foreword; Bishop Vaughn McLaughlin: I have your DNA. Your nickname for me—Fort Knotts—exudes your demand for me to be MORE. Thank you for providing a wholistic example of how I can be, do, and have MORE.

Thank YOU for purchasing this book as it is a sign that my life's pains were not in vain. Legacy is not built without a price. I'm prayerful that my price will discount your pain and problems and increase your prosperity.

TABLE OF CONTENTS

Foreword

Put this book down right now if you are not ready for truth! I'm talking about "truth" that confronts you, "truth" that concerns you, and "truth" that will set you free from issues, insane ideologies, retarded belief systems and principles that you have lived by and with for years . . . yet wondering why life is not better!

Put this book down right now if you are not ready to become challenged mentally, spiritually, physically and socially. If you want to think, be and behave as you have been doing for the past "forever", then don't read this book. But if you are tired of your yesterday and your today, then read on! Pastor Knotts has something to say.

Somehow, through the course of his life, his academic journey and his spiritual walk; Pastor Anthony Knotts has written this book that will 'over-turn' how you see yourself, how you view life in general and how far you want to go in this world and the world to come before you close your eyes in eternal sleep.

I was so amazed and impressed at the same time that God in his grace, mercy and love would allow me to walk with such an insightful young man. Pastor Knotts has taken the worst of his past to create the best of his future. Viewing life through the lens of his many experiences, I found myself with fewer excuses and compensations for who I am and what I do than ever before.

Thank you, Pastor Knotts for being transparent. Thank you, Pastor Knotts for studying *"to show yourself approved"* that you might even approach helping all of us know that there really is M.O.R.E. There really is truth in the statement *"we are more than conquerors in Christ Jesus".* There really is truth that I am *"created in the image of God"* with the same creative and loving power of God. There really is truth that my past cannot hinder my future. While the greatest enemy of my destiny, is my history . . . through Christ I can rise above my history and walk tall, strong, sure and confident in my purposed destiny. Thanks for reminding me of all these truths and more . . .

Are you still holding this book . . . still listening to the tape, good let's go. You are headed for MORE and surely MORE is exactly what you shall receive!

Dr. Wanda A. Davis
Author, Preacher, Musician, Counselor

INTRODUCTION
I CAN BE M.O.R.E.

April 4th 1991—the day my whole life turned around. I received a call that my son, Teland Todd, had just been born. "If I liked" I could come and see him. I know "If I liked" sounds strange. What father wouldn't want to see his newborn child? However, it was a reflection of how low I had sank in life.

Three years prior I was scoring touchdowns and getting a great education at Guilford College in Greensboro, North Carolina, a college that I had worked so hard to get into. Before that I was finishing up high school at Lexington Senior High in Lexington, North Carolina. There I was, a starting running back on two back-to-back state championship football teams, vice president of my high school student body, and a three star letterman in two other sports. I was also an over-achieving student in spite of suffering with dyslexia. I'd managed all that while being raised in a household with an abusive, alcoholic father who, caused me to hate weekends.

It's really amazing how your life can turn for the worse when you lose focus of your goals and your inner drive to be more. I had worked so hard to overcome my life adversities. This included heeding the advice and encouragement of special people like Billy Burnette, Steve Weeks, Larry Atkins, Charlie England, Bert May, Becky Griffin, Larry Beck and Garrett "Uncle Bo" Knotts. These were all people who looked beyond my pain and saw my potential to be more, do more, and have more.

Despite all this support, I was somehow able to mess up my whole life and disappoint so many people who had invested so much in me. Now here I was with a new baby boy, while still a boy myself.

As I entered Community General Hospital I was nervous. It wasn't simply that I had not been there for Teland's mom while she was pregnant. This was the first time I had set foot in the place since I'd spent three days in the psychiatric ward. Between hitting rock bottom and the added stress of Teland being born, I'd tried taking my own life. I finally got myself together to go visit my newborn son. I can remember it as if it was yesterday. I walked over to the window of the room where they kept all the babies. I couldn't believe my eyes when I saw him. God had used him to create life just as I'd tried to take my own. As I stood there I could only tell myself "You Can Be More." I had to improve in order for my son to be, do, and have more.

That was the beginning of my pursuit to be, do, and have MORE. I would love to tell you that from that date everything got better. But as often happens, things got worse before they got better. I ended up becoming homeless. I physically assaulted my mother, and she put me out. As I look back it was only by the grace of God she didn't kill me. Instead she did the very best thing she could ever do for me. She gave me over to God. Like the prodigal son in the Bible, I had to hit rock bottom before coming to myself.

Let me just tell you that such a blessing can also come to you. On January 24th, God sent his messenger, Darin Jones, a saved spirit and basketball player from Livingstone College, to wash clothes at my sister's house. He shared a message of hope with me unlike any I'd ever heard.

He told me that God loves me and that Jesus Christ died for me. Most importantly, he said God had MORE for me to do and that through Jesus Christ I could be MORE. The next day I gave my life to Jesus Christ and I have been walking with Him since. Teland is now twenty and a redshirt junior on football scholarship at UNC Pembroke. I am married to the love of my life, Byrdzetta H. Knotts (my Rachel). Together, we have two beautiful kids, Jalen and Destiny. I pray that as you read this book you will be encouraged to invest in yourself and understand that in spite of adversity and negativity you can be, do and have MORE in life.

CHAPTER 1
YOU CAN BE M.O.R.E.!

The Japanese have developed the most dynamic and prosperous economy in the world since the close of the Second World War, with the help of a business philosophy from American William Demery) called *"Kaizen."*

Kaizen essentially means "continuous improvement". Japanese companies made it their number one priority to constantly improve their products, services, and business processes. The dominant question in the minds of Japanese executives and managers was and still is, "How can we improve on these products, services or business processes?" The effectiveness of this way of thinking is evident in the success of the Japanese economy and the availability of Japanese products and services throughout the world.

Over the years companies who employ the Kaizen approach have managed to develop and maintain a strategic advantage over their competitors. On the other hand, the majority of those companies that do not make continuous improvements inevitably go out of business. This book is all about a Kaizen approach to Being, Doing and Having MORE in Life. Your life is your business and your main business is your life. In order to maintain your own advantage in life and be more, you must make continuous improvement a major priority. An approach that can make a country like Japan, among others, successful can work as well with any individual that embraces this philosophy.

Personal Improvement is not an Option; it's Imperative

In Japanese the word is pronounced "ky-zen". Kai means "change in action to correct", while Zen means "good". So quite literally, Kaizen means "an action to change for the good" and "to make something better in one's own eyes". Kaizen aims to improve productivity in life by minimizing and eliminating waste. I think this is the solution to many problems that we face in our world today.

The Chinese translation supports my thinking. It is worth noting that while extremely similar to the Japanese, the Chinese translation adds "benefit" to the definition of the word. In this regard, the term "Kaizen" refers to positive change that not only triggers the improvement of individuals, but also society as a whole. Kaizen, from the Chinese perspective, concentrates on improving society by improving the individual. Everyone is a valued contributor to the success of society and must therefore be given the necessary education, tools and encouragement to contribute on a continuous basis. in his or her way.

Personal improvement is not an option; it is imperative. It is simply the process by which you become stronger spiritually, mentally, physically, and financially. It is the never-ending quest and commitment to becoming all that you can be (MORE), fueled by a firm belief in your own potential. Those who are committed to personal development believe that they can perform better and get better results if they are better conditioned to do so. They have, therefore, committed to a process of lifelong conditioning through personal improvement.

Continuous personal improvement can't be achieved if you don't invest in yourself. We live in a time where people want fast—and they want it for free. You have to be willing to invest in yourself before you expect someone else to do so.

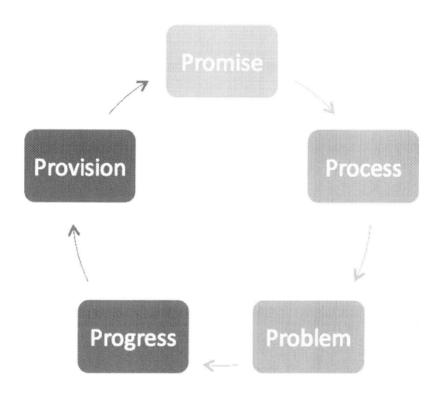

Every minute that you spend reading personal development books, listening to personal development audio/video programs, participating in seminars and workshops, prayer and meditation, working out at the gym and worshipping at church amounts to a wise investment in yourself. Over a period of time these kinds of investments will yield a remarkable return because you did more so you could have MORE.

The opposite is also true. The failure to invest quality time, money and effort into your own personal growth to become more will eventually exclude you from the opportunities that the future holds. Your best and most profitable investment is the one you make in yourself to be MORE. I recommend that you invest at least 10% of your time and money into your own education and personal development.

I RECOMMEND THAT YOU INVEST AT LEAST 10% OF YOUR TIME AND MONEY INTO YOUR OWN EDUCATION AND PERSONAL DEVELOPMENT

Take time out for yourself, spend money on yourself, and do things for yourself. By doing so, you will avoid a future collision with regret. Regret is perhaps one of the most painful human emotions. It hurts because it points an often unnecessary finger at you and blames you for whatever is going wrong. Regret says "If you had taken a different road back then you wouldn't be hurting so badly now."

Regret blames you and beats you up for wasting time, money and energy. I wrote You Can Be MORE not only to help you avoid the collision with regrets, but also to contribute to you getting MORE results out of life. So invest in yourself NOW and know that Byrdie and I believe that you can be MORE.

I.R.A. (Identify issues, take Responsibility, Action plan)

1. In what areas of my life have I settled for less than the best? Why?

   _____
   _____
   _____
   _____
   _____
   _____
   _____
   _____

2. What can I do to improve in these areas?

   _____
   _____
   _____
   _____
   _____
   _____
   _____
   _____
   _____
   _____

3. How will I accomplish this improvement?

   _____
   _____
   _____
   _____
   _____
   _____
   _____
   _____

Regret blames you and beats you up for wasting time, money and energy.

CHAPTER 2

M.O.R.E. ADVERSITY

"If thou faint in the day of adversity, thy strength is small."

—King Solomon

In June of 2007, Byrdie and I had the thrill of a lifetime. We were given two free tickets to attend the NBA finals game between the Cleveland Cavaliers and the San Antonio Spurs. LeBron James and Tim Duncan—I could not believe my eyes! What was even better was that our tickets were box seats five rows behind LeBron's mom. They also gave us backcourt access to all the free food and drinks we could consume. While back there we saw some of the past NBA greats, like Patrick Ewing, walk by our table. All of this was possible because we had the right admission tickets.

One year later, however, I found myself facing one of the greatest tests of my life. This time pain, suffering, stress, and other difficulties were the price of admission. Like the experience of the NBA finals, I could not believe my eyes. Life seemed to be on the rise; yet so many positive things had happened the prior year.

Now two years after that personal life Katrina, I pondered the following statements and questions: In a world without hurdles there are no champions. Without suffering there are no saints. Without battles there are no victories. Without rain there are no rainbows. Doesn't it appear that a world that includes pain is more rewarding than one that doesn't? Isn't heat necessary to produce gold, pressure and polishing necessary to produce diamonds, and adversity necessary to produce my character? Absolutely!

> A WISE PERSON RIGHTLY SAID THAT ADVERSITY INTRODUCES A MAN TO HIMSELF.

I discovered after that period of adversity (not the NBA finals) that even under the worst circumstances we can choose to focus on the positive rather than the negative. Thomas A. Edison is a great example. In 1914, a fire almost destroyed his New Jersey laboratories. Valuable records of his experiments and two million dollars worth of equipment were lost. After surveying the damage, the sixty-seven year old Edison said "There is great value in disaster. All our mistakes are burned up. Thank God we can start anew."

Let me ask you a question. Do you feel that with each step forward, adverse circumstances pull you two steps back? If so, you're not alone. Most people feel the same way. A wise person rightly said that adversity introduces a man to himself. You have to decide how much suffering your pain is going to inflict upon you and those around you. Here are a few ways of thinking that will help you turn adversity into a positive experience.

Adversity is a Symptom, Not a Cause

Often adversity is a symptom of some other deeper problem. Maybe you just lost your home, and you feel lost amidst the devastation. But do you try to figure out why you lost a home? What made you so susceptible to the mortgage crisis? Was it really the right time for you to purchase? Similarly, if you or a loved one is sick, is it due to lifestyle or eating habits? Is it simply your attitude? As physical pain is often a symptom of some malady, your adversity may also be a symptom of another problem. Although your first priority is to handle the current situation, you should make a mental note to ascertain the real of the source of the problem. Unless you solve it, you will keep getting into similar situations. Remember: every problem has a solution.

Adversity is a Teacher

Sometimes adversity comes to your life to suggest a change in direction. Dr. Wanda D. Turner stated in her book, **Celebrate Change,** that "complications are those painful things that God allows into your life at those junctures where change is not an option. It is mandatory."

When someone leaves your life, business, or church there is no use sulking and blaming yourself or frankly, even the other person. At one point when people began to leave the church I pastor, I spent so much time talking about the people who had left that I forgot about the ones who remained. Then one day one of my new sons from the ministry, came to me and politely said, "Pastor, will you please stop talking about who left and start teaching us who are still here."

What a wake-up call. John Churton said, "In prosperity, our friends know us; in adversity, we know our friends." Confucius once said, "I was complaining that I had no shoes till I met a man who had no feet." This is so true. Rather than getting bogged down with our own problems we should pay attention to people who happily survive—and even prosper—despite all odds. When we open our eyes and take a look at the larger world, we will be happy to know how well life has treated us. We then realize it could be worse and count our blessings.

When a mother eagle believes her eaglets are large enough to learn how to fly, she begins to take apart the nest and push the eaglets out. After this rude awakening, the eaglets discover they have wings! They can fly! I now realize that God uses the adversity in our lives for the same purpose. He wants to nudge us, pushing us off one cliff after another, in the hope that one day we too will discover our wings and soar to new heights.

IN PROSPERITY, OUR FRIENDS KNOW US; IN ADVERSITY, WE KNOW OUR FRIEND."

Adversity is like standing before a grave. It can make you come alive or it can bury you. Dealing with adversity is never easy. Yet conquering the adversity will give you confidence, inspire others, and make you ready for the next challenge in your life. Understand that adversity is like rain and the sun. It will fall and shine on all the same. Rich or poor, black or white, old or young—all will experience adversity at some point in life. Adversity is part of life. So don't fight it; accept it.

Adversity is Inevitable

It is simply naïve to think that you can walk through life or embark upon a project without some form of adversity. Positive action always seems to attract adversity. In fact, the ability to anticipate adversity is one of the key skills necessary to overcome it and move on to MORE.

For those who maintain a positive outlook on life, adversity can be a builder. But to the negative thinker, adversity is nothing but a MORE blocker. People who desire to be MORE, do MORE or have MORE operate by Murphy's Law. This law states that "Anything that can go wrong will go wrong, and at the worst possible time." It is designed to take the naïveté out of the planning process, so that planners and pursuers of MORE can:

1. Anticipate it

2. Avoid it (if possible)

3. Answer it (developing solutions to problems before they arrive)

But isn't Murphy's Law rather negative? No! Anticipating problems is only negative if you use it to justify poor planning or procrastination.

If, on the other hand, you use it to develop advanced solutions, then it is nothing short of being proactive.

Adversity is Conquerable

William Thompson, my mentor, says every problem has a solution. This means all adversity in life can be conquered instead of it conquering you. What you believe about conquering adversity will determine how hard you look for the answer. If you believe that it can and must be conquered, you will not stop seeking the answer until you find it. For example Morris D. Rouff invented Formula 409 after 408 failed attempts. He treated each failure as a learning experience. What do you think kept him going in spite of 408 failures? It was his belief that all adversity in life can be conquered and there is an answer.

Adversity is Beneficial

There is a mysterious blessing hidden in all adversity you face. The gift of power always comes securely wrapped up in adversity. If you conquer adversity, you get the power. It's that simple. Adversity survivors are problem solvers. Problem solvers become more powerful with each problem solved because they acquire new knowledge and skills. With each victory their self-esteem rises and with it, their confidence.

It is as though your hidden potential and creative genius are asleep inside of you waiting for a problem of sufficient magnitude to come along and wake up the Adversity is Incredible Hulk within you. There part of life. is a glorious purpose for all adversity you face. When you understand the purpose of the adversity you can harness its power. There is a fourfold purpose of your adversity. It is . . .

ADVERSITY IS PART OF LIFE. SO DON'T FIGHT IT; ACCEPT IT.

To Empty Out Hidden Potential In You: Hidden within you are the most incredible capabilities, concepts and creativity. However, your inner genius will never be known until the right kind of pressure forces it out. Your adversity serves to bring out of you a new dimension of competence, conceptualization and creativity that you would not have otherwise known. One of my favorite scriptures in the Holy Bible is Proverbs 24:10, which states "If you faint in the day of adversity, your strength is small." Adversity reveals to you that there is MORE power in you.

To Energize You: There are only two great energizers in life, pain and pleasure. Adversity comes along whenever we get lethargic, lazy, casual or indifferent, and spurs us to stop wasting time because it hurts. In this way, adversity can strengthen your resolve to achieve goals and pursue MORE. Adversity may feed your faith, strengthen your beliefs and reinforce your personal values. There are some moves you will never make in life until the pain of staying put outweighs the potential pain of taking action to be MORE, do MORE, and have MORE.

To Educate You: In the process of finding answers to adversity, you will acquire new knowledge and skills for yourself. You will discover, develop and began to demonstrate things about yourself you didn't know before the adversity. Often the adversity will drive you to people, places and even prayer to gain information in which you would not otherwise have been interested. The adversity, in this way, educates you because it pushes and prepares you for MORE.

To Elevate You: Once you have been emptied, energized and educated you are processed for promotion. Going into the adversity you just had the mindset of survival, but because you endured it you are

> EVERY PROBLEM HAS A SOLUTION

qualified for elevation. When I played running back on the 1985 and 1986 2A state championship Lexington Senior High football teams, one of my favorite Coaches, Charlie England, would always say, "No pain, no gain." Interestingly enough, he would always say it when we were running a conditioning drill called "County Fair". This was a drill in which the pain was so intense we all wanted to just puke and quit. But somehow we managed to persevere through and it helped make us repeat state champions!

I am an avid reader. Recently I purchased John Calipari's book, **Bounce Back**. I didn't purchase it because I'm a Kentucky Wildcat fan (I love my North Carolina Tarheels). What caught my interest was the title and especially the subtitle, "Overcoming Setbacks to Succeed in Business and in Life." The timing of this book could not have been better.

I was just getting motivated again after a two year period during which the church I pastor had gone through serious transition. I called it my "Titanic" period because so many people were jumping overboard. As if that was not enough, the business in which I had invested my family's life savings went belly up.

> WHEN YOU UNDERSTAND THE PURPOSE OF THE ADVERSITY, YOU CAN HARNESS THE POWER OF IT.

I can't remember what I was looking for that day I went to the bookstore. But what I found gave me the push I needed to keep striving, to bounce back. In his book, Coach Calipari talks about seeing the bottom of life from two very distinct and very public setbacks and personally learning that bad situations are only permanent if you allow them to be.

He went on to explain that in 1999, he was fired from his job as head coach of the NBA's New Jersey Nets twenty games into his third season. This incident left him publicly humiliated and emotionally devastated.

Coach Calipari never allowed the negative to overcome him or those around him, and he began plotting a course for his first bounce back. It was a journey that took him to the University of Memphis and, in 2008, to the NCAA's main event, the men's basketball Final Four.

That trip ended in a crushing overtime loss in the title game, as he watched his team lose a nine point lead with two minutes and twelve seconds left in regulation. However, this time armed with the knowledge and fortitude he had gained in overcoming the Net's firing, Calipari began his second bounce back.

One year after that defeat, Calipari was named head coach of college basketball's all-time winningest program: the University of Kentucky Wildcats. In ten years, he went from his lowest low to landing his dream job at a dream program. Coach stated, "Its not about how far you fall but how high you rebound or bounce back."

Coach Calipari recognized adversity for what it is, an opportunity to lift yourself to a higher level and experience your bounce back. While going through my personal adversity test, I realized that I had three ways to respond:

1. The response of an egg: when you drop an egg on something hard it breaks on the outside. Some people allow themselves to become all broken up in life. I call that wearing their feelings on their sleeves.

2. The response of an apple: when you drop an apple on something hard it bruises on the inside. Some people allow themselves to become an emotional wreck internally.

3. The response of a tennis ball: when you drop a tennis ball on something hard it doesn't break or bruise, it just bounces.

My adversity really showed me that I had a tennis ball mentality. I could bounce back regardless of how low or how hard I fell. Today, the church I pastor is healthier than it was before. In addition, my business has recovered to the point that we have clients in the USA and the UK. Now that's a bounce back! If it can happen for me it can happen for you. Get ready for your bounce back!

I.R.A. (Identify issues, take Responsibility, Action plan)

    1. What adverse situations have I encountered in my life?

_____

_____

_____

_____

_____

_____

_____

_____

    2. What role have I played in the adversity I have faced?

_____

_____

_____

_____

_____

_____

_____

_____

    3. How can I utilize adversity to make me a better person?

_____

_____

_____

_____

_____

_____

_____

_____

IT'S NOT
ABOUT HOW
FAR YOU FALL
BUT HOW
HIGH YOU
REBOUND OR
BOUNCE BACK.

CHAPTER 3
M.O.R.E. GOALS

Mark McCormack's book, *What They Don't Teach You* at Howard Business School, tells of a Harvard study conducted between 1979 and 1989. In 1979, graduates of Harvard's MBA program, were asked whether they had set clear, written goals for their futures and made plans to accomplish them.

The study showed that only 3 percent of the graduates had written goals and plans; 13 percent had goals, but not in writing, and 84 percent had no specific goals at all, aside from getting out of school and enjoying the summer.

In 1989, 10 years later, researchers re-interviewed the members of the class. The study showed that the students who had unwritten goals (13%) were earning, on average, twice as much as the the students who had no goals (84%). Most impressively, they found that the graduates who had clearly written goals when they left Harvard (3%) were earning, on average, ten times as much as the other 97% of graduates altogether. The only difference between the groups was the clarity of the goals they had for themselves when they graduated. Wow! Talk about the power of goal setting.

When you really think about it, our entire life is all about goals. Without goals one does not thrive in life; one simply survives. You can only achieve MORE in life when you are purposefully recording, rehearsing and reviewing your goals.

WHY PEOPLE DON'T HAVE GOALS

If goal achievement is automatic, why do so few people have clear, written, measurable, time-bound goals that they work toward each day? This is one of the greatest mysteries of life. Goals allow you to change your life by empowering you with vision and expectations to take control. Unsuccessful, unhappy people usually talk about their problems and who or what is to blame for their situation. Successful people keep their thoughts and conversations focused on their most heartfelt desired goals. Their thoughts and speech usually focus on what they want. They understand that they are in control of achieving their goals and being MORE in life. I believe there are six reasons why people don't set goals:

SIX REASONS PEOPLE DON'T SET GOALS

1. They don't understand the importance and value of setting goals
2. They fear criticism of others
3. They fear failure
4. They fear success and the responsibility that comes with accomplishing set goals
5. They enjoy familiar surroundings
6. They have never been showed how to properly set goals

> WITHOUT GOALS ONE DOES NOT THRIVE IN LIFE; ONE SIMPLY SURVIVES.

When you understand that your life is based on at least four simultaneous dimensions, the Spiritual, the Personal, the Physical and the Financial, you can begin to develop a strategy that factors in each. This starts by creating a vision for each of the four dimensions.

Right now I would ask you to get a pen and four sheets of paper. At the top of each sheet, write one of the following: Spiritual, Personal, Physical and Financial.

Under each heading on each sheet, write down everything you would like to become, achieve, possess or experience on this dimension. Let your imagination go! Don't limit yourself! Remember, though, that any goal is realistic with a realistic time frame. Don't worry about the size of your goal; just be true to your deepest desires. It may be that some of your goals won't be reached for another twenty years. That is perfectly okay. Just write down everything you would like to become, achieve, and process on each dimension.

REALISTIC TIME PERIOD

The next step is to link each goal to a specific time frame. Next to every goal, write an expected date of achievement. This will add a sense of reality and responsibility to the goal. For example, if you give yourself three months to reach a certain goal, your brain will say to itself, "We only have three months to make it happen." It starts getting excited and begins generating both the strategies and the energy necessary for the achievement of your goal.

> GOALS ALLOW YOU TO CHANGE YOUR LIFE BY EMPOWERING YOU WITH VISION AND EXPECTATIONS TO TAKE CONTROL.

Without the time frame, your mental genius lies dormant because it assumes you're not serious about achieving the goal. It is like the difference between someone casually, saying "We should get together some time" or saying, "I would like to meet with you this week—how about Friday at 4p.m.?"

The two messages send different signals to your brain. The first one provokes no response and requires no action. The second provokes an immediate response and requires action. The same is true with your goals. They must be set in such a way that they provoke an immediate response and require immediate action. The way for this to happen is by attaching realistic time-frames to your goals.

Goals without deadlines are really wishes. There is a profound difference between the two. Most people have wishes but few people have goals. Wishes describe the things you would like to become, achieve or possess. Goals describe the things you intend to become, achieve or possess. Your wishes only become goals when you decide to make them come true. Wishes do not require much mind power, but goals do.

WHAT ARE THE ROAD BLOCKS TO YOUR GOALS?

Your next task is to write down the thing or things that prevent your achieving each goal. This is quite simple when you understand that technically there is mainly one of two reasons why we do not achieve a goal:

1. We don't know what to do
2. We don't do what we know

With each goal write whether it's ignorance (don't know) or inactivity (won't do) holding you back. This task will help you to identify the roadblocks of your future success, and also give you an outline of how to achieve it. If you are already motivated but don't know what to do, then your goal is to seek out those "in the know" for answers.

LET YOUR IMAGINATION GO! DON'T LIMIT YOURSELF!

PRIORITIZE YOUR GOALS

The next step in developing your life plan is to group all of your goals into one of these categories:

long Range Goals—These are your big picture, long-term goals and describe the main outcome you desire in life. They pertain to your overall life mission and personal values, and constitute things that are most important to you and form your personal legacy. For example, becoming an expert in your field is a long-range goal. The happiness and security of your family is a long range goal. Making it to heaven is a long range goal.

mid Range Goals—These constitute the things you need to do consistently in order to achieve your long range goals. For example, running a business is a midrange goal, as are physical training and fitness. These goals are basically a means to an end.

Short Range Goals—These are the things that must be done initially in order to make your mid range goals possible. For example, if it is your mid range goal to practice piano regularly, your short range goal is to start taking lessons. If your mid-range goal is to have multiple streams of income and stay out of debt, your short range goals are doing some research, finding a financial mentor, opening some accounts, and developing a budget.

The system works when you start with long range goals and allow them to determine mid and short range goals. You do this by asking a series of strategic questions:

1. What do I want to become, achieve and process in my lifetime on all four dimensions of my life?
2. What do I have to do consistently or well in order to achieve my long-range goals?
3. What must I do right now to make it to the mid-range stage?

These three categories can also be thought of as phases of progress toward the end result. By systematizing your goals in this way, the path toward them becomes clearer.

I.R.A. (Identify issues, take Responsibility, Action plan)

1. What roadblocks have hindered my goals and aspirations?

   _____
   _____
   _____
   _____
   _____
   _____
   _____
   _____

2. Why have these roadblocks become bigger than my goals?

   _____
   _____
   _____
   _____
   _____
   _____
   _____
   _____

3. How will I approach my goals differently in order to achieve them?

   _____
   _____
   _____
   _____
   _____
   _____
   _____
   _____

Wishes do not require much mind power, but goals do.

CHAPTER 4

M.O.R.E. TIME

*"Don't count every hour in the day, make every
hour in the day count."*—UNKNOWN

Time is a powerful God-given resource—invisible, unchangeable and unstoppable. Everyone has the same amount of time each day. Everyone must live on 86,400 seconds, 1440 minutes, or 24 hours each day. That's 168 hours a week, or about 691,200 hours in a lifetime if a person lives to be 80. Each segment of time received must be spent instantly and effectively to be, do and have MORE. Don't fall into the trap of thinking that your time constraints are unique and unmanageable. It doesn't matter where or how you're currently living—whether in the projects, in a gated community or anywhere in between. The one constant is that no matter who you are, or where you are, your ability to be MORE in life will depend on how you invest the 24 hours you're blessed with each day.

If you're willing to seize the initiative, you can learn time management just as you can learn to use a cell phone, play the organ, or master any other skill you desire. The more ambitious you are, the better you must be at squeezing every last ounce of usefulness out of every minute at your disposal. Whether or not we choose to admit it, many people are busier than we are and still find time to accomplish MORE. They obviously don't have more time—they just put their time to greater use. You can do the same.

> THE ONE CONSTANT IS THAT NO MATTER WHO YOU ARE, YOUR ABILITY TO BE MORE IN LIFE WILL DEPEND ON HOW YOU INVEST THE 24 HOURS YOU'RE BLESSED WITH EACH DAY.

The thing I love about time is that it doesn't discriminate. It doesn't care about color, race, class, what your parents did, or who you think you are. Each and every day starts with a clean slate. No matter what you did yesterday today begins anew. Everyone, this includes you, has the same access and opportunity to make the most of time to be, do and have MORE.

"Time is free, but it's priceless. You can't own it, but you can use it. You can't keep it, but you can spend it. Once you've lost it you can never get it back."—Harvey MacKay

Being MORE in life is a direction, not a destination. So long as you are making consistent progress towards a personal goal you are succeeding at being MORE. Every day that opportunity must be embraced with passion. Each new day brings with it a world of possibilities. You must greet it with both expectation and enthusiasm. With the proper use of time, you can become something, achieve anything and do everything that God put you on this earth to do. Purpose is why you were created, and time is the period you are given to discover, develop and demonstrate that purpose. I have put together seven keys to effective time management:

KEY #1 to time management is to re-evaluate time itself.

How valuable is your time? People in the world seem to fall into two distinct categories—"Time Wasters" and "Time Chasers". The "Time Wasters" most often have no goals and no desire to be, do, and have MORE. The "Time Chasers" have goals and an inward passion to be, do, and have MORE. They understand that the moment you establish a goal your time becomes that much more valuable.

The value you place on time is always in direct proportion to the value you place on your goals and your desire to be MORE. Time is only important if your goals are important. Time is only essential if your goals and desire to be MORE are essential. When re-evaluating time, make your time as precious as your goals.

KEY #2 to time management is to develop the habit of goal setting.

Start everything with the end in view and start nothing until you know what you hope to achieve. Our divine Creator implemented this technique when He created the earth. Isaiah 46:10 mentions "declaring the end from the beginning." From now on, everything in your life must start with targets, goals, objectives, desired outcomes or required results. Begin each day with a clear mental picture of how you expect the end of the day to look. Remember, if you aim at nothing specific in life, you hit your target every time. Before going to bed at night, take a few minutes to determine your desired outcomes for the next day. This causes you wake up in the morning mindful of your goals. If you don't know where you're headed, any road will take you there.

KEY #3 to effective time management is the ability to overcome distraction.

Distractions come in many shapes and sizes and they all can break your focus and waste your time. Any unsched-uled intrusion is a distraction. There is a difference be-tween a distraction and an obstruction. An obstruction may require problem-solving skills, while a distraction will require the power of focus. Whenever you are in motion it is imperative that you watch where you are going, because

> DON'T FALL INTO THE TRAP OF THINKING THAT YOUR TIME CONSTRAINTS ARE UNIQUE AND UNMANAGEABLE

you will flow in the direction of your focus. In the Bible Peter was successful in walking on water until he took his eyes off his goal and focused on what he had already overcome—the wind. How many times do we begin to pursue our goals but something comes and seizes our attention? Like Peter, we end up falling because we were distracted. You cannot complete a task effectively while focusing on something else.

This may also include the temptation to multi-task. This temptation is always there. However, refusing to start a second task until the first is completed has proven to be a more effective time saving technique. Multi-tasking guarantees activity, but it does not always deliver productivity. Working on a task does not make you productive, whereas completing one does.

KEY#4 to effective time management is to develop the art of time saving.

This means finding quicker ways of achieving the same quality of result. This art is developed through what I call the "Do It", "Defer It", "Delegate It", or "Drop It" technique. "Do It" means you must complete it yourself, and now. No procrastination. "Defer It" means you must do it, but it can be delayed. "Delegate It" means you must properly convey the sense of urgency to someone else with the proper skills to handle it. To delegate a task to someone lacking the proper skills is called "dumping". The last part of this technique is "Drop It". This means that the task has no bearing on the outcome of your goals, and is not worth yours or anyone else's time.

KEY #5 to effective time management is to cultivate the habit of writing out your thoughts, whether on paper or electronically.

There is a difference between a goal and a task. A goal describes the desired outcome. A task describes the activities that must happen to produce that outcome. Before going to sleep at night, ask yourself this question: What must I do tomorrow to accomplish what I want? Make a list and work throughout the day to complete the tasks.

KEY #6 to effective time management is to develop the habit of prioritizing your tasks.

All your tasks are important, but some are more important than others. These are usually the ones that relate to your values and vision for life. These may include faith, family, fitness, finances, friends, and/or even things you want to achieve. The key is to keep the important things important by doing them first.

KEY #7 to effective time management is to employ a daily systematic formula that monitors and records all your activities.

FOUR THINGS YOU
CAN DO WITH TIME

SPEND IT	WASTE IT
USE IT	LOSE IT

I.R.A. (Identify issues, take Responsibility, Action plan)

   1.   What are some distractions in my life?

_____
_____
_____
_____
_____
_____
_____
_____
_____

   2.   What have I done to contribute to these consistent distractions?

_____
_____
_____
_____
_____
_____
_____
_____
_____

   3.   How will I take control of my time?

_____
_____
_____
_____
_____
_____
_____
_____
_____

TIME IS FREE, BUT
IT'S PRICELESS.
YOU CAN'T OWN
IT, BUT YOU CAN
USE IT. YOU CAN'T
KEEP IT, BUT YOU
CAN SPEND IT.
ONCE YOU'VE
LOST IT, YOU CAN
NEVER GET IT
BACK.

CHAPTER 5

NO M.O.R.E. PROCRASTINATION

"Procrastination is the art of keeping
up with yesterday and avoiding today."
—Wayne Dyer

P rocrastination is the needless postponement of completing tasks—especially out of habit. Everyone has experienced it. While for some people it is a minor irritation, for others it is a way of life that produces much stress and anxiety. Some individuals thrive on the pressure of tight deadlines, but procrastination is about more than just time management. It is often based on a false sense of security and lowered expectations.

Procrastination is the vampire of a productive life. It will suck the life out of any worthwhile endeavor. Therefore it is very important to realize how counterproductive procrastination can be in an environment where you must stay motivated in order to accomplish your goals. So why do people procrastinate?

Overload and Inability to Prioritize

Assignments may seem too difficult and you begin to look for ways to avoid them. Your "To Do" list keeps growing and you start to feel overwhelmed. Whether it's home life or work life, you begin to feel as though you will never catch up. You feel like you don't know where to start which induces panic. You suddenly realize that you are falling so far behind that you are tempted to give up. This cycle can become paralyzing.

Poor Time management

The task may seem too time-consuming, so you put it off until "later." There is always "later", right? You may become overconfident and underes-timate the actual time need-ed to complete all your obli-gations. You may even think about your time without taking into account upcom-ing assignments, extra time needed to seek help, or time needed for short breaks to refresh your mind.

PROCRASTINATION IS THE VAMPIRE OF A PRODUCTIVE LIFE, AND WILL SUCK THE LIFE OUT OF ANY WORTHWHILE ENDEAVOR.

Fear Of Failure or Fear Of Success

Fear is a very strong driving force. Sometimes you fear you will fail at something that is very important to you. Sometimes you fear success because of what that could mean. The outcome is the same. Fear of what will happen frightens you so much that you don't work to achieve your goals.

Assignments may require knowledge or skills you don't think you have. This makes them intimidating. Fear of failure prevents your even attempting the task. It is easier to rationalize failure by neglecting assignments.

Boredom

Sometimes the work is not challenging enough to hold our attention. Focusing on the outcome (the bigger picture) will help keep up your motivation to do the work.

An unchecked habit of procrastination is like a bottle of spoiled milk: the ingredients do not ripen to their full potential, and in the end you are left with a bitter taste in your mouth. The habit can cause stress and feelings of regret.

Procrastination is a habit that is quickly formed and hard to break. It starts when a person continuously chooses the path of least resistance, or prioritizes activities with instant gratification. Putting off an otherwise easy activity makes it harder, and putting off something difficult can make it impossible.

Large goals tend to have delayed gratification. For example, I put off exercising by choosing to spend time sleeping and watching TV instead. The reward of weight loss or muscle tone from exercising cannot be seen or felt instantly, whereas I felt relaxation from watching TV right away.

PEOPLE WHO ARE AFRAID TO FAIL ARE USUALLY AFRAID TO EVEN ATTEMPT THE TASK.

Putting off small activities related to a larger goal may not allow for the full achievement of the end result for which you were striving. Even putting off seemingly unrelated activities can affect larger goals.

For example, the goal of starting your own business and the activity of working out seem unrelated. But indirectly one can effect the other. Working out can not only improve your overall fitness level but also give you increased energy to focus on your business. Highly effective people may also use the time spent working out thinking about their business. Alternatively, an unrelated activity such as watching TV would not help the overall goal. Non-productive activities, in moderation, can be a good thing when the mind and body need downtime. Moderation is the key.

Have a Positive Attitude

One of the greatest hindrances to overcoming procrastination is a negative attitude. Be positive and open minded about assignments. Begin to build confidence and a sense of satisfaction by sticking to a daily study routine and finishing tasks for the day. Most importantly, get the help needed from family members, pastors, mentors, accountability partners, and support groups. Overcoming procrastination requires a change of attitude. Successful people know there is a better chance of reaching a goal when it is approached with a positive attitude.

YOUR ATTITUDE IS A CHOICE

Attitude is a choice. Many people tell themselves that they will increase their chances of success if they wait for all the circumstances to be "right" before tackling a project. This thought process often leads to procrastination.

Success means making a decision to do regardless of what the circumstances say.

Successful people are not always those with the greatest natural ability or the highest IQ. Those who consistently reach goals successfully have a positive attitude and believe they can reach their goals.

Thinking about how you might have responded differently to a problem in the past is an important part of being a better problem-solver today. Moderation here is important as well. Analyze what you could have done differently and chalk it up to experience. Remember, you cannot control the past so move on. An ounce of now is worth a pound of later.

The Dangers of Procrastination

lowered Self Confidence

Procrastination feeds into feelings of low self-esteem. The stress of not keeping up with assignments and not accomplishing tasks on a daily basis will damage your sense of achievement and well-being.

Using Procrastination as a Coping mechanism

Delaying action may give the feel of coping with pressures. However, delay actually adds to your stress level and makes it much more difficult to feel good

LARGE GOALS TEND TO HAVE DELAYED GRATIFICATION

about managing the work load. Procrastination then becomes a very inadequate way to cope with the pressures of timely completion of assignments. It also adds a sense of guilt.

A False Sense of Your Ability to learn Effectively

Procrastination seriously undermines your ability to do your best. Once on the merry-go-round of procrastination, the worry of keeping up and being bombarded may cause you to lose sight of what you're actually learning, affect your ability to finish assignments and to thoroughly and reliably learn the material.

A Sense of Powerlessness

You begin to feel as if you have no control over your ability to get things done. This will seriously affect your commitment to stay motivated and accomplish your goals.

Procrastination Interferes With Opportunities

You are not acquiring the training and skills needed to succeed when all your time and energy is consumed with avoiding work. Sometimes, as mentioned before, we avoid training because we recognize the likelihood of it leading to success. Precious new opportunities may be passing you by.

Dealing with Procrastination

Realizing the considerable discipline required to get everything done that needs to get done each and every day is an adjustment process. It is also one of the biggest realities facing people who want to be, do, and have MORE. Part of the adjustment process is learning how to stay focused and make the best use of your time. How can you avoid some of the pitfalls of falling behind in reaching your goals? You can do this by:

> THOSE THAT CONSTANTLY REACH THEIR GOALS SUCCESSFULLY HAVE A POSITIVE ATTITUDE.

- Having clearly defined **goals**
- Setting **priorities**
- Having the **motivation** and **discipline** to follow through
- Reinforcing your **desire** to achieve

Goals are desired achievements and the purpose toward which your work is directed. Priorities are those things that are of greatest importance to you. Motivation is the commitment to accomplish your purpose and to keep going even when things get difficult. Discipline is the systematic intention and conscious choice to focus on accomplishing your goals. Each of these is interconnected.

**Goals » Priorities » motivation » Discipline:
a constant desire to achieve**

Even if your goals and priorities are clear, your motivation and discipline can be adversely affected by procrastination.

Detoxing From Procrastination
Take Small Steps

If you find your work too challenging, take small steps. Break the work into smaller and more manageable components. Be organized. Learn to plan ahead. Organize your work schedule in a manner that allows you to accomplish a bit more each day. Take pride in each day's achievements. The task may be hard by the yard, but inch by inch it is a cinch.

Start Today

Don't deal with procrastination by procrastinating! Saying, "I'll face up to the issue tomorrow or the next time," may be easy, but it's extremely important to make every day count. Remember, the only way to break a bad habit is to just do it—like ripping off a band aid. The end of the year comes very quickly and you will have to live with the results.

Prioritize

How many times have you read that already in this book? There may be a dozen tasks to complete. Put them in order of importance. Avoid always choosing the easiest task first. It will most likely lead to procrastination. Be efficient with your time. Allow for breaks. These are very important in easing your stress level.

Be Aware Of Your Choices

Pay close attention to your immediate response and your attitude when given an assignment. Be aware of your first choices.

Do your best to fight the urge to avoid doing the necessary work for completion of the planned assignment. Take note of your feelings as you choose to tackle the work needed to get things done. Make a list of your responsibilities. Be clear as to where you need to take care of business. Remember these important considerations for balanced living—management of class time, study hours, the job, recreation, socializing, household chores, personal errands and rest.

Set a goal every day. List the tasks necessary for completion of the goal. Be realistic about the time needed for each task. Keep track of where your time goes. Be sure to identify and secure the ideal study environment. Eliminate distractions. You will be amazed at how much you can accomplish when your attention is truly focused.

The Benefits of Overcoming Procrastination

Kicking the habit of procrastination offers many benefits—peace of mind, a healthy feeling of strength, purpose and being in charge of your life. Remember, procrastination is self-reinforcing. Every time you put off doing something it reinforces a negative attitude toward that task.

Knowing how procrastination works and how you can greatly reduce its influence in your life, will allow you to experience a greater sense of freedom and personal satisfaction. You may still procrastinate once in a while. Keep working on it. Now you will be much more aware of it and be able to more quickly resolve the situation. When you do succeed, take time to enjoy your success. Remember it the next time you need encouragement. Allow it to build confidence in your abilities.

I.R.A. (Identify issues, take Responsibility, Action plan)

1. In what areas of my life do I often procrastinate? Why?

    _____
    _____
    _____
    _____
    _____
    _____
    _____
    _____

2. How have I stunted my progress as a result of procrastination?

    _____
    _____
    _____
    _____
    _____
    _____
    _____
    _____

3. What steps can I take to eliminate procrastination in these areas?

    _____
    _____
    _____
    _____
    _____
    _____
    _____
    _____
    _____
    _____

PRIORITIES
LEAPFROG OVER
ONE ANOTHER,
EACH TRYING TO
ASSERT ITS NEED
TO BE ATTENDED
TO FIRST.

CHAPTER 6

M.O.R.E. BALANCE

*"Happiness is not a matter of intensity but of balance
and order and rhythm and harmony."*
—Thomas Merton

Certain areas in life—spirit, mind, body, social relationships, finances, church, career—are important for everyone. However, the degree of importance for each of them may differ. But being able to have a specific focus in each of the areas enables us to achieve a healthy balance. That balance will, in turn, empower each area again, preventing any area from dragging you down.

A balanced life is certainly one of the most important overall goals to reach. Achieving it can be tough. Focus on something you want to achieve, on the one hand, allows you to make progress. On the other hand, you may tend to lose focus in another area. So how can you balance the important areas of your life and still achieve what we want?

One answer is the development of a wider perspective. This is a multi-step process. First, you will need to take a step back and decide what are the important areas. Second, you have to make sure that you maintain this perspective. Finally, do not allow yourself to become lost in any one area, turning your back on all the others. Defining those areas of importance creates an awareness of what matters to you. This allows you to make a huge step toward balance.

Pressure to succeed, time lines to meet, and an ever-changing environment challenge us all to stay light on our feet. On any given day, we need to handle all the essentials of our jobs and attend to the multitude of occurring crises. Priorities leapfrog over one another, each trying to assert its need to be attended to first.

Balance is the key to leading a successful and beautiful life. It is important that everyone maintain a balance between the various aspects of their daily routine. My son, Teland, a junior in college, has experienced a rude awakening in this area. Balancing his studies, the football team, a part-time job and fraternity activities has been a battle. His failure to find balance could result in failure in all areas.

I, too, as a pastor, must know how to balance my personal life. Failure to find a balance between family and church, trying to maintain happiness in others' lives while neglecting my own, may result in burnout.

It is equally important that we maintain a balance between materialistic and spiritual life as well.

Work-life balance is not about choosing between work and personal life. Nor is it simply about equally dividing your time between the two. Sometimes we assume that there is one formula for doing this. We should realize that what leads to balance today might be different tomorrow. Here are some ways to find balance between your work and your personal life.

Set Your Priorities

As stated before, one of the difficulties faced as we start to find a balance between work and personal life is focusing on too many priorities. We want to be good parents, a perfect husband or wife, and still strive to come out on top of the corporate or entrepreneur world. The best way to set priorities is to order things in terms of significance. This allows you to focus more time on your top priorities. I know this first hand after trying to juggle all my roles. As a result, I came to a great understanding by looking at my hand.

YOU SHOULD PROTECT YOUR FREE TIME FIERCELY

1. My thumb represents my personal relationship with Jesus Christ

2. My pointer finger represents my partnership with my wife

3. My middle finger represents my parenting of my children

4. My ring finger represents me being a pastor because a shepherd is married to his sheep

5. My pinky finger represents my professional life, because it's my ability to earn money to take care of the first four

Try to cut back on unimportant activities that steal valuable time from your top priorities. Activities such as unproductive after-work gatherings or meeting old acquaintances may not help you reach your goals in life. Other activities, such as Facebook and watching TV, should be minimized to allow you more quality time for your personal life. I have also found that learning how to say "no" to people or things that are not aligned with my passion will free up time.

Your FREE Time Should Be ME Time

Your free time is your time spent not working. This is where you can enjoy being with yourself and being by yourself. It's also where you can make a big difference in reaching your goal of a work-life balance. This is a time of personal refreshment.

Protect your free time fiercely. During your free time, be care-ful not to think about work, your current to-do list, or future commitments. Just enjoy living in the moment. In our home I have a special time when I can be "King For The Day". I get to sit on my "throne", the couch, and relax. No obligations. No children. No chores. No cooking. Just "King Anthony" for the day. What a Life!

YOUR FREE TIME SHOULD BE ME TIME

Keep Yourself Organized

This is an area I am still trying to master. A clutter-free life means that you are in control, whether in the office or at home. It is easy to prioritize, adjust, and enjoy life when you are not bogged down by the confusion and stress that comes from being disorganized. Organize your desk and your schedule. If you see something you don't need, trash it. Afterwards, you will feel better and more in control.

Live and Work In Your Passion

A fast way to achieve a work-life balance is to love and be satisfied with what you do and who you are. The Apostle Paul told the church at Phillipi, "Whatever state that I am in, I have learned how to be content."

Much of your time will be spent at work. It will be difficult to be happy with your life if you don't love what you do. Keep a positive attitude toward your work and enjoy doing what you know best. This will only yield great results as you strive toward your business goals. In addition, you will also achieve happiness in your personal life.

There Are Four Techniques to Improve Balance in Your life

1. You can stop doing certain things altogether. There are many things you are doing today that made a lot of sense when you started them in the past. But today,

KEEPING YOUR LIFE CLUTTER-FREE MEANS THAT YOU ARE IN CONTROL

they are ideal candidates for "the trash can of your life." You can save several hours out of the day or week just by discontinuing certain activities altogether. I stopped playing golf, for example. After all, I only made it through nine holes and I was horrible at it!

2.   You can do less of other things. Ask yourself what things you should be doing less of if you want to simplify and gain balance over your life, family, and business. At one point I stopped trying to collect money from our non-paying clients. I delegated that to my wife, and we have since seen a greater retention of clients.

3.   You can do more of certain things. What are the things that you should do more of to improve balance in your life, family, or business? Once I stopped dealing with collections, for example, I spent more time doing what I love to do: selling and recruiting.

4.   You can start doing something new. What new things do you need to undertake to solve problems, overcome your obstacles, and achieve your goals? What immediate shifts should you make to begin working on these new tasks and activities to improve balance in your life? Often, one simple shift in the direction of a new goal can simplify and bring balance to your life.

Setting up Boundaries— and Staying Within Them

Setting healthy boundaries is essential for a healthy worklife balance. Sounds true, but what does it mean? What do healthy boundaries look like? How can you know where and how to set them? Well, here's an personal example. I decide that I will not arrive at the church before a certain time, and I won't work later than a specific hour.

I advise you to consider not working through lunch. Schedule lunchtime just like any other appointment. Decide day by day whether it will be for your relaxation. Examine your boundaries, and observe whether they are giving you room to live or cramping your style.

Stop Being a Workaholic

Workaholism has become a serious problem for many people, especially pastors. In fact, according to the latest numbers from the International Labour Organization, U.S. workers put in an average of 1,815 hours per year compared to major European economies where hours worked ranged from around 1,300 to 1,800. It is clearly a disorder, on par with alcoholism or addiction to gambling. Being overworked may cause creativity, productivity, communication, and cooperation to drop off a cliff. Workaholics typically continue to work passed the point of exhaustion. This may cause them to make mistakes. They may then feel the need to work even harder to fix the mistakes. Statistics show that many pastors are resigning because of burnout and the effects the job are having on family relationships.

> WORKAHOLICS TYPICALLY CONTINUE TO WORK PAST THE POINT OF EXHAUSTION, CAUSING THEM TO MAKE MISTAKES AND WORK EVEN HARDER TO FIX THEM.

Finding it difficult to take some time off? Remember it's a process. Start slowly. Begin with leaving the of-fice early one evening. Then take a full day off. Try leaving the cell phone at home when you are going out with the family. Also, focus on what you do best. Think about what other talents you have outside of work and make time to do them. Once each year, I take a whole month off from being a pastor. I don't go to the church for the entire time.

Simplify Your life

Think about your values. Which are most important? Spending time with family? Accumulating great wealth? Achieving powerful influence? Acquiring possessions? Expressing yourself? Learning new ideas? Experiencing adventure and travel? Maintaining excellent health? Socializing with friends? Contributing to the community?

You can't do them all. Write down the ones that really matter to you. Cut out activities that aren't consistent with your core values.

Tips For Achieving Balance:

THE FASTEST WAY TO ACHIEVE A WORK-LIFE BALANCE IS TO LOVE AND BE SATISFIED WITH WHAT YOU DO AND WHO YOU ARE.

Create a written plan. Think about what you could and should be doing as it relates to your priorities. You determine you want to have an amazing relationship with your family. What does that mean? How, specifically, are you going to make that happen? Spending more time with them must become a priority. This means reserving special family time to make certain you are staying connected with what is going on in their lives. Write this into your schedule! Byrdie and I have date night once a week, as well as a family night.

Living in balance is the object of life. Learning how to keep things in our lives in balance is one of the lessons we must learn. We are to live in a manner that ensures all of our priorities are given proper attention. Progressing through life in this way, the right manner, assures feelings of the highest satisfaction and confidence. We will be free of doubts that something is being neglected. For example, concerns that we are not spending enough time with family and friends will be erased. We will have arranged things in our life in an ideal order that allows us to give some attention to each of our priorities.

Be on the lookout for extremes. There will be things that will try to suck you in and consume the majority of your attention. You will have to make certain you don't fall into the trap. Don't allow yourself to take anything to the extreme. Refuse to focus on only one thing in lieu of other priorities in your life. Obsessively focusing on only one priority, for example, working all the time, will never allow you to achieve balance. In addition, it will be the cause of your missing out on other things. Remember, excuses only please the people that make them. Don't try to rationalize why you can't have balance in your life.

Don't fall into the trap of believing that it has to be one thing or the other. There is room for everything you determine as priority. Your objective is to determine how it all works together. Refute all excuses, especially the one that says, "It just isn't possible".

DON'T TRY TO JUSTIFY THE REASONS YOU CAN'T HAVE BALANCE IN YOUR LIFE.

Use idle time better. Don't waste any time. Figure out how to use downtime productively to focus on one of your priorities. When I have a long commute in between appointments, for example, I call my clients, prospects, family, or friends. Sometimes if I have a half hour before my next meeting, I will use that time to relax and clear my mind by meditating or taking a nap. Be creative. Use your idle time in a good way.

No false deadlines. Although you want to make progress in each of your priority areas, be realistic about what you can do on any given day. Always ask yourself if it's really necessary to complete a given task by "X" date. Give yourself the time you need to accomplish certain tasks so that you can make certain you have time to focus on all of your priorities. Don't convince yourself that you have to meet deadlines that don't really exist.

Review your progress and priority list every day. Take note of how you are doing so you can make the necessary shifts. Are there things you just never get to? Are there certain areas you spend way too much time doing? Make certain you understand what is working and what is not. Switch things around if necessary.

I.R.A. (**I**dentify issues, take **R**esponsibility, **A**ction plan)

1. In what ways is my life out of balance?

_____
_____
_____
_____
_____
_____
_____
_____

2. What activities or people cause imbalance in my life?

_____
_____
_____
_____
_____
_____

3. How can I begin creating a more balanced life daily?

_____
_____
_____
_____
_____
_____
_____
_____

THE MOST
IMPORTANT
INVESTMENT
WE PUT INTO
ANY GOAL OR
RELATIONSHIP
IS NOT WHAT
WE SAY, DO, OR
HAVE. IT'S
IN WHO WE
ARE.

CHAPTER 7
M.O.R.E. SELF-ESTEEM

"Until you make peace with who you are, you'll never be content with what you have."—Doris Mortman

S ome of life's great lessons suggest that before we can achieve success in the world around us, we must first achieve success within ourselves. The most important investment we put into any goal or relationship is not what we say, do, or have. It's in who we are. I spent many years of my life trying to win the approval of people who either weren't interested or had nothing to offer. It brings tears to my eyes thinking about the time, money, and energy I spent trying to get people to accept and approve of me. That's the danger of not knowing who you are. I found out quickly that if you don't know your identity other people will give you theirs.

The world's fastest growing crime is identity theft. Identity theft is a crime in which an imposter obtains key pieces of someone else's personal information in order to impersonate them. Often this may be the person's Social Security numbers or driver's license number. While I never took anyone's Social Security or driver's license number, I did find myself sort of borrowing their identities because I didn't like myself. I thought I could find identity through those I hung around.

I found an interesting thing about disliking myself. I realized that I felt about the same when I was the pastor of one of the fastest growing churches in Greensboro and driving my dream car as when I hit rock bottom and was riding around on a ten speed bike. What was this feeling? Emptiness.

After experiencing these flip sides of life and ending up with the same feeling of emptiness, I realized it was more than not knowing my identity. I had a serious case of low self-esteem.

Low self-esteem is difficult to detect. But it is a major deterrent to being, doing, and having MORE. Our sense of self-worth determines how well we function in every area of our lives. This emits from our feelings and behavior to our careers and relationships. Our self-esteem shapes our attitude toward life. It determines whether we face the adversities of life with a "Yes, I can be MORE" or a "No, I can't be MORE" attitude. I have come to realize that our self esteem is either the launching pad of our victories or the trap that triggers our failure.

Knowing how we became the way we are means understanding the sources of our damaged self-esteem. This is a major step toward becoming emotionally whole and healthy. As we grow stronger and more secure in ourselves, we become happier and have a greater impact on those we love.

THE SOURCE OF MY IDENTITY AND SELF ESTEEM ISSUES

At birth, our identity and self-esteem is a clean slate. We have no reason to think we are inadequate. We are not comparing ourselves to those around us. Soon after birth, we are exposed to experiences that shape us emotionally and mentally. We receive messages. They may be subtle and overt, verbal and nonverbal, intentional and unintentional, loving and abusive. These message experiences, if not checked, begin to help form our identity and self-esteem.

Looking back over my life I realize these messages are powerful. They tell us who we are and how we are viewed by oth-ers. This is especially true of how we believe we are viewed by our parents. For me, growing up in a household with an abusive, alcoholic father had profoundly negative effects on my identity and self esteem. For as long as I can remember, my father repeatedly would tell me that I was nothing and I never would be anything. Knowing what I know now I realize that my father suffered from low self esteem, because those that make it a point to hurt others are usually in pain themselves. Unfortunately, for me and for so many others, hindsight is always 20/20.

> OUR SENSE OF SELF-WORTH DETERMINES HOW WELL WE FUNCTION IN EVERY AREA OF OUR LIVES, FROM OUR FEELINGS AND BEHAVIOR TO OUR CAREERS AND RELATIONSHIPS.

There is one incident that haunted me for years. My father was physically assaulting my mother and I jumped in to rescue her. He was smoking a cigarette. As I joined in the altercation, he removed it and literally put the cigarette out on my forehead. Now, not only did I have to deal with the verbally abusive words ringing in my head, but I also had the visible signs of his abuse on my head. I was eight years old when this happened. I would spend the next thirty years car-rying these tormenting experiences with me. Consequently, I became very bitter and insecure. I categorize this experience in the following manner:

1. Unhealed hurts—what shouldn't have happened in my life but did
2. Unmet needs—what should have happened in my life and didn't
3. Unresolved issues—the explanation of the first two was never explained

I have no illusions that in both healthy families, as well as, unhealthy families children will have unavoidable experiences that damage self-esteem. Mistakes and abuse can happen outside of the home as easily as inside the home. In a healthy family, these messages of inferiority will tend to be minimal and will be counteracted by messages of love, acceptance, approval and affirmation. In less healthy families, such as mine, even when one parent is positive the profound negativity is what dominates the child's soul. Regardless of where they are encountered, these experiences will chip away one's self esteem. The more pain experienced, the more one is hindered in releasing his or her hidden God-given potential. A damaged identity and low sense of self worth hampers one's ability to:

1. develop enough courage to face the adversities in life with confidence and motivation;

2. develop social intimacy with other people;

3. develop intimacy with God.

THE SYMPTOMS OF LOW SELF-ESTEEM

The following are some of the characteristics frequently found in people with low self-esteem and identity issues. As you read through these traits, you may recognize yourself or someone close to you.

Compensating behavior—Persons with low self esteem fre-quently seek to compensate for their emotional pain through substance abuse, working, people-pleasing, compulsive sexual behavior, or other mood-altering behavior. This was a major problem for me in my high school years. In my attempts to gain friends. I would act outside of the values that my mom instilled in me just so people would accept me in their cliques. This is how I began drinking and smoking marijuana—to cope with the pain of my home life—hoping that my friends would give me the love I should have been getting at home.

> SOMETIMES YOU CAN CELEBRATE SCARS BECAUSE YOU HAVE THE MEMORY BUT YOU DON'T FEEL THE PAIN.

Intolerant or judgmental comments about other people—Persons with low self esteem frequently try to displace their self-hatred onto others through critical or caustic criticism. They may tend to react with anger or annoyance to the very flaws in others that consciously or subconsciously remind them of themselves. For example, an individual who hates himself for an inability to complete a certain task may be exceptionally critical of other people who can't complete that same task in their lives.

Self-consciousness—Many persons with low self-esteem will become highly irrational and antagonistic when they perceive themselves as being criticized by others. They may be excessively over-concerned about what others think of them, and become easily embarrassed. After my father put that cigarette out on my forehead I didn't want to go outside because I feared what my friends would say.

Perfectionist attitudes—These persons often compensate for their feelings of inferiority by demanding perfection from themselves or other people, especially a spouse or children. The individual accepts other people conditionally and only if the performance is "good enough". Unfortunately, the performance is rarely "good enough".

Depression—Persons experiencing low self-esteem often demonstrate pent up anger, guilt, and self hate which frequently lead to depression. Symptoms of clinical depression include anxiety, sadness, disturbed sleep, inability to concentrate, indecisiveness, increased or decreased appetite, withdrawal, painful thinking and suicidal thoughts. Depression was one of the factors that caused me to end up in the psychiatric ward after trying to kill myself. My personal identity and self-esteem was shot to pieces.

False pride and arrogance—Persons with low self esteem often feel that the way to pull themselves up is to put others down. Such a person will actively belittle people around him, exercising intimidation and controlling behaviors, all in an attempt to keep others in a lower position. This makes the person feel like he or she is on top. People with low self esteem may over-emphasize competitiveness, possessing the best, or being the best.

TIPS TO IMPROVING YOUR SELF-ESTEEM

One's self-esteem is largely formed (for better or worse) by childhood experiences. However, there are a number of significant tips that can be taken to rebuild and remold self-esteem. Using these tips can aid in living life with a MORE positive and accurate assessment of yourself and the ones you love.

TIP #1—**Avoid putting yourself down.** Mistakes are a part of being human. Accept your humanity, forgive yourself, and get on with your life. I often say to the people I pastor and mentor, "Mistakes corrected become wisdom."

TIP #2—**Avoid the envy trap.** Envying another person's abilities, appearance, accomplishments, possessions, status, opportunities, or income is a guaranteed self-esteem beat-down. Your aim should be to become satisfied with what God has given you. Recognize and accept the person He has molded you to be. Always be committed to growth and increasing maturity.

Several years back I found myself being jealous of a local pastor whose church was growing faster than mine. Every time I heard his name or saw him, something burned inside of me. This pastor had not done anything to me. In truth, he didn't even know I felt this way about him. I prayed and asked God to help me overcome those feelings of envy and jealousy. God told me to announce to our church that I would be attending the pastor's bible study one Wednesday night, and that I wanted them to

> OUR SELF-ESTEEM SHAPES OUR ATTITUDE TOWARD LIFE AND DETERMINES WHETHER WE FACE THE ADVERSITIES OF LIFE WITH A "YES I CAN BE MORE" OR A "NO I CAN'T BE MORE ATTITUDE.

accompany me. Wow, what an impact! Not only did our church show up in large numbers, but God also led me to give a financial seed to this ministry from our church—directly to the pastor. We enjoyed the service and I got free from the envy that I carried in my heart.

TIP#3—Be proud of the unique, special person God has created you to be. When you hate yourself, you are really blaming God for making a mistake. God doesn't make mistakes. As you learn to accept yourself, you will be able to experience a closer relationship with God and others.

TIP#4—Think, speak, and act positively. Replace such messages as "I can't . . . " or "I have to . . . " with messages that say, "I can be MORE and I will be MORE."

TIP#5—Replace negative self-talk with positive self talk. What we repeat to ourselves over and over is self talk. Learn to replace these negative assumptions with positive statements. As you do this, these negative messages are gradually erased as your self-esteem grows.

Thirty years later, after enduring the horrible experiences with my father, I can proudly say that he is no longer an alcoholic. He is a born again Christian. The first time I saw him again was after his being away for over twenty years. He came to hear me preach. He told me afterwards that he was proud of what I'd become. Not bad coming from a man who had told me I would "never be nothing". After that service I went home and looked into the mirror and began to celebrate the scar on my forehead. Sometimes you can celebrate scars because you have the memory but you don't feel the pain.

I.R.A. (Identify issues, take Responsibility, Action plan)

1. What areas of my life have been invaded by low self-esteem?

_____
_____
_____
_____
_____
_____
_____
_____
_____
_____

2. In what ways have I discounted my uniqueness?

_____
_____
_____
_____
_____
_____
_____

3. How can I change my perception of myself?

_____
_____
_____
_____
_____
_____
_____

We can speak
with our
mouths at a
rate of 150
to 200 words
per minute,
but we carry
on an inner
dialogue with
ourselves at
an astounding
rate of about
1,300 words per
minute.

M.O.R.E. POSITIVE
SELF TALK

W e can speak with our mouths at a rate of 150 to 200 words per minute. But we carry on an inner dialogue with ourselves at an astounding rate of about 1,300 words per minute! This inner dialogue is called self-talk. The question is what are we saying to ourselves in this fast speed internal conversation we have with ourselves? The messages we repeat to ourselves in the self-talk process are often negative and self-defeating. Most of our self-talk is unconscious and undirected. It often reflects an illogical and painful assumption we have built up about ourselves and about our lives.

These negative messages often lead to low self esteem, obsessive-compulsive behavior, depression and anxiety. They often appear as lack of confidence, and distortions in our relationships. Unconscious self-talk tends to overemphasize events and importance on what other people think and say about us. Or in some instances, what we think they say about us. Sounds like paranoia, right?

And there we saw the giants, the sons of Anak, which come of the giants: and we were in our own sight as grasshoppers, and so we were in their sight.

Numbers 13:33

This scripture really reveals the power of negative self-talk. Not only did the ten spies have negative self-talk, but it caused them to form an image of themselves as to how the giants viewed them. This was done without ever having a conversation with the giants. Needless to say, the spies did not reach their promised land even though they had a piece of it in the cluster of grapes that they captured before their return. Negative self-talk will always cause you to settle for a piece of what God created you to have instead of the full portion.

Cognitive psychologists such as author and founder of *Rational Emotive Behavioral Therapy*, Dr. Albert Ellis, have identified the types of "irrational" thinking that forms the basis of negative self-talk. Here are a few examples:

Focusing only on problems: This means complaining and focusing only on what's wrong, rather than on what could be done to solve the problem.

Catastrophizing: Everything that goes wrong is a catastrophe! We expect the worst and magnify problems.

Blaming: Instead of looking for a solution to the problem, we look for someone to blame.

When you tell yourself you can't handle something (or some other self-limiting thought), you tend to stop looking for solutions. For example, notice the difference between telling yourself you can't handle something and asking yourself how you will handle something. Doesn't the second thought feel more hopeful and produce more creativity? Negative self talk tends to be a self-fulfilling prophecy!

The first step toward change is to become more aware of the problem. You prob-ably don't realize how of-ten you say negative things in your head, or how much it affects your experience. The following strategies can help you become more conscious of your internal dialogue and its content.

> YOU ARE BORN WITH THE LABEL OF A CHAMPION; IT IS THROUGH NEGATIVE SELF-BELIEF AND SELF-TALK THAT YOU TURN YOURSELF INTO A LOSER.

- **Journal Writing**: Whether you carry a journal around with you and jot down negative comments when you think them, write a general summary of your thoughts at the end of the day, or just start writing about your feelings on a certain topic and later go back to analyze it for content, journaling can be an effective tool for examining your inner process.

- **Thought-Stopping:** As you notice yourself saying something negative in your mind, you can stop your thought mid-stream by saying to yourself "stop". Saying this aloud will be more powerful, and having to say it aloud will make you more aware of how many times you are stopping negative thoughts, and where.

- **Accountability Partner:** Another self-improving strategy is to ask for help from someone who has your best interest in mind. Ask them to correct you every time they hear you say something that is negative or not life producing. Since we function in many roles, you may seek the assistance from several people.

- Positive affirmations are a great tool to reprogram your unconscious mind from negative thinking to positive. The idea is to take positive statements about what you would like to see manifested, and repeat them enough so that they're part of your way of thinking and seeing the world. This operates in the same way that negative self-talk does, but in a way that benefits you. To come up with your own positive affirmations, use the following guidelines:

> YOU ARE BORN WITH THE LABEL OF A CHAMPION; IT IS THROUGH NEGATIVE SELF-BELIEF AND SELF-TALK THAT YOU TURN YOURSELF INTO A LOSER.

• Look at your intentions: Think about what you are trying to create in your life, which means the end product, behaviors, attitudes, and traits you would like to see yourself develop in order to get there. Would you like to feel more peace? Would you like to live a healthier lifestyle? Would you like to be a more supportive spouse or more successful in business? You might want to brainstorm what's important to you and get to the heart of what you want to create in your life.

- **Create statements:** Once you get an idea of what you're aiming for, try to put that idea into a few simple statements that reflect the reality of what you want to create. Phrase the statements as if they are already true, not that you would like them to be true. For example, the affirmation, "I am successful in business each day," would be better than, "I want to be successful in business every day." This is because you are programming your subconscious mind to believe the statements, and that helps manifest them into reality. You're not trying to want something; you're trying to make it so. Deloris Williams, a member of my church, created her positive affirmation statement that I really enjoy. She says, "I will increase my wealth, maintain my health and encourage myself."

- **Be sure they're positive:** When making positive affirmations, be sure they're positive! This means saying what you want to see and experience, not what you don't want to see and experience. For example, instead of saying, "I'm tired of being in debt," or even, "I hate debt," use, "I'm financially free". Sometimes your mind doesn't register the negative, and it just hears the concept, "debt", which is what you're trying to avoid.

- **Make them realistic:** Your subconscious mind can benefit from positive affirmations that stretch and expand your perspective, but if you push things too far, your inner judge steps in and negates the affirmations. Be sure that you're making your affirmations realistic, but hopeful as well, and positive affirmations will work for you. For example, the affirmation "every day, in every way, I'm getting better and stronger" might feel like too much of a stretch, and your subconscious mind might beg to differ. However, saying "I am learning from my mistakes," or "I am grateful for all that I have in my life," might feel more real to your subconscious mind. Experiment, and see what feels right to you.

You are born with the label of a champion; it is through negative self belief and self talk that you turn yourself into a loser. When David went up against Goliath in the bible, he wasn't thinking negatively. He only spoke and walked in what he believed God to do, and God did it. Do you believe that you can have all you want, become what you want to be, go wherever you want to go and touch as many lives as you want to touch?

Self talk acts as a small voice within you, quietly encouraging you and spurring you on to greatness in your everyday tasks. Walk and talk in that awareness. Don't be ignorant of who you are and what your purpose is in life. Remember there is always a light at the end of the tunnel.

I.R.A. (Identify issues, take Responsibility, Action plan)

1. What is the root of negativity in my speech/ conversation?

    _____
    _____
    _____
    _____
    _____
    _____
    _____
    _____

2. How often do I allow negative thoughts to become negative speech?

    _____
    _____
    _____
    _____
    _____
    _____
    _____
    _____

3. How can I replace negative thoughts with positive thoughts?

    _____
    _____
    _____
    _____
    _____
    _____
    _____
    _____

Confidence
is simply a
matter of
believing in
who you are
as a person.

CHAPTER 9
M.O.R.E.
CONFIDENCE

S tudy the lives of many of history's most successful people and you will find that they have achieved their incredible outcomes because they mastered one simple, yet incredibly powerful attribute. This attribute was the key to achieving the impossible dream for people like Benjamin Franklin, Thomas Edison, Harriett Tubman, Thurgood Marshall, Bill Gates, Martin Luther King, Michael Jordan, Magic Johnson, John Maxwell, President Barack Obama and of course, Jesus Christ. Unfortunately, less than one in a thousand people fully utilize it! The good news is that it can be learned and used by anyone, regardless of background, education, or IQ. I'm talking about the attribute called confidence. Being, doing, and having MORE in life (and helping others do the same) begins with confidence.

Confidence is simply a matter of believing in who you are as a person. Confidence is integral to success in your life because it gives you the strength to achieve your goals. However, confidence is not feeling superior to others or putting other people down in order to feel better. In fact, people with the most confidence have an uncanny ability to see the good in the people around them and to encourage them in their endeavors without jealousy. All confident people share several characteristics.

For a moment, let's have a look at the common characteristics of confidence.

Self-belief

Confident people simply believe that they can succeed and do what they set out to do. They are able to define goals for themselves and to take steps to obtain them. Their self belief allows them to rise to any challenge. Believing in your self is a powerful force—motivating and empowering you to succeed.

Assertiveness

All confident people have the courage to be assertive enough to stand up for themselves and their beliefs. Even if their opinion is considered unpopular, confident people will stand up for what they believe in. Being assertive isn't about being aggressive or bullying. It is about stating what you think and sticking to your own beliefs, not being swayed by what other people think.

Optimism

Confident people have a realistic view of their future. They can recognize that even bad situations will eventually right themselves and that difficulties can be overcome with sensible plans. They have the ability to see the light at the end of the tunnel and plan their journey toward it. Optimism allows confident people to believe that they will be okay, no matter how bad the current situation looks.

Liking yourself

Learn to love yourself. Confident people have realistic self-images. They can look at themselves and find things they like. They don't focus on the negative, instead realizing the things that they do well. However, they also recognize aspects of themselves on which they have to improve. Through improving these things they become stronger and more confident.

Taking responsibility

Confident people have the courage to take responsibility for their own actions. When they make a mistake, they own up to it and admit they are wrong. They have the ability to learn from their mistakes and make the changes needed to avoid the same mistakes in the future. That in turn increases their self confidence. This often reveals the leader when working with a group of people because when things go right the leader gives the credit to others but when things go wrong the leader takes the responsibility.

> CONFIDENCE, SELF-ESTEEM OR SURE KNOWLEDGE OF WHO YOU ARE COMES FROM SELF-INSPECTION.

Complimenting others

Confident people have the ability to see the good and positive things about the people that surround them without feeling jealous. They will celebrate the accomplishments of friends rather than get angry about them. Confident people tend to stand out from the crowd, have better personal relationships, and perform better at school or work. If you find yourself lacking confidence, it is a great idea to take a look at the confident people around you and to mimic some of their behavior.

Finally, compliment the people around you without jealousy to create long lasting positive relationships. These are the actions of a confident person who is sure to be successful and happy at whatever he does. That is the real strength you get from knowing what is confidence.

There are certain characteristics possessed by those who have high self esteem and confidence in their ability to affect the journey of their life. These factors are universal and can be learned if they are not present in your life right now:

They are ambitious. They want more from life than existence or survival. They can envision themselves in better circumstances and surroundings.

They are goal oriented. They seek the challenge of completing and setting new goals for themselves. They are not especially competitive, except against themselves. They enjoy breaking their own records.

They have learned to communicate. They know how to ask for what they want and to hear advice and counsel. It is less important for them to be right than to be effective. They listen more than they speak.

They are loving and kind. Those people who have a good inner self image form nourishing relationships instead of toxic ones. They have learned to detach from relationships which do not allow them to be authentic.

They are attractive and open to others. Self confident people are usually drawn to one another. They vibrate their confidence in a way that attracts good things and good people to them. Being attractive does not necessarily mean physically attractive in the usual sense of the word, but rather spiritually beautiful.

There are also universal characteristics of those who have low self esteem and lack the confidence to attract to themselves abundance in all areas of life. These factors, which often negatively influence the joy that a person may experience are:

Fear of change. Many people who lack confidence come from a basis of being without, and live their lives in fear of "what if?"

Difficulty communicating what they really want from life. This includes unclear ideas of what is valued and muddled goals and desires.

Wanting to please others more than be true to themselves. The desire to have peace at any price is more important than discovering personal potential. They resemble chameleons, changing to fit the current environment.

Insecurity and being drawn to others who also see themselves as victims. Destructive and toxic relationships that reflect and increase feeling of lack of self-worth are formed.

Confidence, self esteem or sure knowledge of who "I am" comes from self inspection. It is an intimate experience and resides in the core of one's being. The hardest labor ever done in life is internal work. There is no greater barrier to strong, healthy and mutually respectful relationships than lack of confidence.

Nothing is more important than healthy self-esteem and confidence, both for you and the other person if you hope to achieve a happy relationship. No greater barrier or roadblock exists in relationships than the deep-seated feeling that one is not loveable or worthy.

I.R.A. (Identify issues, take Responsibility, Action plan)

1. Who or what in my life diffuses my confidence?

_____
_____
_____
_____
_____
_____
_____
_____

2. How have I contributed to improving or decreasing my confidence?

_____
_____
_____
_____
_____
_____
_____
_____

3. What can I begin doing today to increase my self-confidence?

_____
_____
_____
_____
_____
_____
_____
_____

CHAPTER 10

M.O.R.E. HOPE

There is a source of perpetual mental and emotional fuel available to aide in the achievement of personal dreams. It is called "HOPE". Hope is far more tangible and powerful than a wish. It is a well developed and confident belief that a specific vision (goal, dream—a promise) will be achieved or fulfilled within a specific timeframe. Sustaining any genuine hope of achievement, or fulfillment is extremely difficult if personal visions or desires are not clearly defined.

Through hope the walk in confidence begins. Hope is the expectation that sustains while waiting patiently for future fulfillment of goals, dreams, and promises. There must be an understanding that hope is about potential (or future) and not past or present. Hope produces progress toward a given goal. Progress produces even more hope and greater momentum.

As each phase of a goal is completed, more hope is produced to help in achieving the next phase. True hope becomes the fuel that keeps you moving toward the ultimate fulfillment of a vision. Mankind's only perpetual energy is Hope.

Hope has a threefold direction:

1. Upward—Hope in God and what God can do.

2. Inward—Hope in who I am and what I can do.

3. Outward—Hope in others, who they are and what they can do.

Hope eliminates the need to compete. The statement is often made, "I wish I were like him or her." We don't understand that saying this is an affront to God. The moment you become "like him or her", there becomes two of "him or her". One of you is no longer necessary. That's why they say opposites attract. Hope allows for an understanding that "I am fearfully and wonderfully made."

Be who you are! Hope eliminates the need to spend time running opinion polls, asking people, "What should I do and how does this look." People will always have something to say about how you should be. But the world needs more people who are going to be themselves. In today's society and churches all over the world, marriages are struggling because the wives or husbands are busy trying to be the ex-girlfriend/boyfriend.

When you have hope you must stay away from:

1. Hope Fillers

2. Hope Stealers

3. Hope Killers

Deferred HOPE

Hope is put off when we fail to take the necessary steps and complete the tasks needed to fulfill our goals. When hope is defined it begins to step away. When hope is put off, emotional energy and motivation is lost. Creativity and productivity begin to decrease. Withdrawal or withholding, sooner or later, means totally giving up on the vision and dream. Give up too many dreams and living becomes little more than just getting by.

Hope Motivates Others

We create seeds of hope in others by stating or employing commitments. Commitments create a vision. Failure to fulfill those commitments in a timely manner defers others' hope. They may lose their motivation, as well as their trust in us. The effects of deferring hope in others may even lead to the death of a relationship.

> IF WE FAIL TO TAKE THESE STEPS AND COMPLETE THOSE TASKS TOWARDS OUR GOALS, HOPE CAN BE PUT OFF.

Hope is shattered when expectations are set too high. When expectations are too low, hope is never created. Refusal to defer the hopes and dreams of those who you are responsible for helping creates loyalty, creativity and productivity. A whole new source of energy is brought into our work, our marriages, and our lives when we stop deferring hopes and begin to focus on helping others fulfill their genuine needs, dreams and desires. Doing so will bring a new dimension of joy and fulfillment into their lives. It will increase their morale, commitment, and trust. Their creativity and productivity will explode!

One of the greatest stories of hope that I have ever seen was shown on ESPN. The story had to do with Anthony Robles. Robles is the Arizona State University wrestler who defeated reigning champ Matt McDonough from Iowa State to become national champion in the 125-pound weight class. A national championship is an impressive achievement for any athlete. It is a more awe-inspiring message of hope when you consider that Robles was born with only one leg.

Clearly one of the keys to Robles' athletic success is his attitude and determination of hope. "I grew up like a normal kid," Robles told reporters. "Yeah I was missing my leg, but that wasn't going to stop me from doing anything I wanted to do." Robles, the oldest of four kids, says his parents played an enormous role in making him feel he had no limits. "My parents really encouraged me. Whatever I wanted to do, my parents were right there behind me pushing me on."

> IF YOUR VISIONS OR DESIRES ARE VAGUE INSTEAD OF DEFINED, YOU CANNOT SUSTAIN ANY GENUINE HOPE OF ACHIEVING THEM.

Robles became interested in wrestling when his older cousin, a high school wrestler, would take him to practices in the summer. One day the coach asked him to jump in because one of the smaller guys on the team needed a training partner. "I've been in love with the sport ever since," Robles said. The rest, as they say, is history. Robles went from being "not very good", as he puts it, to becoming a three-time All-American and one of the top-ranked college wrestlers in the country. Robles not only inspired his teammates and his coaches, he has also inspired thousands of people across the country.

Anthony Robles demonstrates that nothing is impossible with the power of hope. Immediately after the match, when asked by ESPN how he felt about people considering him an inspiration, Robles said, "It's an honor. I didn't get into this sport for the attention. But it's an honor that they consider me like that."

WE CREATE THE SEEDS OF HOPE IN OTHERS BY STATING OR EMPLOYING COMMITMENTS.

I.R.A. (Identify issues, take Responsibility, Action plan)

1. In what or whom have I given up hope?

   _____
   _____
   _____
   _____
   _____
   _____
   _____
   _____

2. Have others lost hope in me? Why?_____

   _____
   _____
   _____
   _____
   _____
   _____
   _____
   _____

3. What can I do differently to restore faith in God, myself, and others?

   _____
   _____
   _____
   _____
   _____
   _____
   _____
   _____

CHAPTER 11

M.O.R.E.
RE-EDUCATION

(This chapter is an excerpt from The Mis-Education of the Masses,
written by my mentor, Wayne Malcolm)

"Personal development is your springboard to
personal excellence. Ongoing, continuous, non-stop personal
development literally assures you that there is no limit to
what you can accomplish".
-Brian Tracy

Mis-education occurs when *"the promise of education is broken by the process of education."* When people make choices, they can only choose from the options that are available to them at the time. The problem is that our perceived options are always limited by our level of knowledge and skill! Miseducation occurs when realistic and sensible options are obscured by expectations for you to go in another direction. The difference between uneducated and mis-educated is that, the uneducated person is uninformed and their ignorance is known to them, the mis-educated person has been misinformed and often mislead and they are unaware of their ignorance. The masses receive little or no financial, leadership, business *or success education, which means that they are fundamentally educated for employment purposes only. Many people fail in education because they don't think that the prize in education is worth the process.*

The answer to mis-education is re-education. However re-education for job independence is not readily available in formal institutions. Actually, it is typically available from mentors and teachers who teach from an experience base. People who achieve job independence are usually happy, and in some cases, desperate to share their knowledge and skills with people who want to learn. That's why they write books, produce audios and run mentoring schemes.

Re-education is always self-driven. It isn't compulsory; it is always voluntary. This deals the deathblow to the old theory that your life can be split into learning years and then earning years. Job-independent people are life-long learners who continue to invest in their own education. They collect relevant books and audios. They attend relevant seminars and workshops. They employ the relevant mentors and coaches. They are constantly growing their knowledge and skill in the subjects that produce success.

To achieve job-independence you must first become a strategic learner.

Here are ten things that strategic learners know.

1. **Strategic learning is voluntary**: A basic education is compulsory in the developed world. Likewise, many organizations provide compulsory professional development for their staff and key workers. However, strategic learning is an entirely voluntary affair. It is self-directed, self-organized, self-financed, self-motivated and self-supervised learning, based on your personal life and business goals. As such, it is only compulsory for the people who are serious about success.

2. **Strategic learning starts with a goal:** The starting point for strategic self-development is a dream or vision of success. Once you are clear about what success means for you, you can begin to identify the subjects and skills that if mastered

will make your success realistic, attainable and inevitable. You cannot begin to design a strategic learning plan until you are clear about what you really want and why those subjects and skills will help you to get more of what you want.

3. **Strategic learning is relevant learning:** Most compulsory education is deemed irrelevant by students because they fail to see how the information will assist them in life or in business. This sense of irrelevance does not happen with strategic learning because you only ever study those subjects and skills that directly relate to your goals, or that assist your efforts for success. This is why we refer to it as strategic learning. Strategy is a military term that basically means a battle plan. Your learning should be part of your personal and professional battle plan, or it is simply a waste of time.

4. **Strategic learning costs money:** Compulsory education is always free and as such tends to be undervalued by the student. Strategic self-development on the other hand is voluntary and must be self-financed. This means creating a learning budget, opening a learning account and investing in your own strategic education. It also means being prudent and shopping around for the best products and services in your field. Strategic learners know that learning can be expensive, and that good advice is not cheap. But they also realize that ignorance costs much, much more.

5. **Strategic learning is the ultimate investment:** Money spent on learning is really an investment that yields actual monetary returns. Studies have shown a direct correlation between money spent on learning and the growth of earnings. The general rule seems to be that if you invest hundreds into your own success education, you get returns in the thousands. Likewise if you invest thousands you get returns in the millions. For example, you may spend thousands on learning how to run a business, but this could eventually yield a return of millions. The general rule is that the more you learn, is the more you earn.

6. **Ignorance is expensive:** Those who spend nothing on personal growth pay a much higher price in the long run in the form of lost opportunities and the lack of professional options. They are usually confined to the bottom of the earning triangle, working in menial or manual jobs and are considered disposable or replaceable by bosses and companies. Whatever dreams they have are really fantasies that are wholly unrealistic and unattainable because they possess neither the knowledge nor the skills necessary to materialise those dreams.

7. **Strategic learning makes your goals realistic:** Any goal is realistic if you acquire the knowledge and develop the skills necessary to achieve it. Whether that goal is to become a billionaire in the next ten years or to transform your body in one year or less. It is all possible if you first find out how it can be done (preferably from those who have already done it) and then develop the skills that are necessary to achieve that result. Knowledge and skills are the only way to turn possibilities into probabilities. The good news is that you can learn anything that you need to know in order to achieve any goal that you set for yourself.

8. **Strategic learning is learning from the experts:** Anyone can develop a theory based on research however theories based on experience are more reliable, realistic and relevant for strategic learners. Strategic self-developers know that a good mentor can be a more effective lever for business success than would an MBA from a university. Most MBA students do not go on to achieve business success even though their professor and textbooks are academically sound. The problem is that their goal at MBA level is primarily a qualification and not a successful business.

> MIS-EDUCATION OCCURS WHEN "THE PROMISE OF EDUCATION IS BROKEN BY THE PROCESS OF EDUCATION."

9. **Strategic learning aims for qualities and not qualifications:** The goal in traditional education is a qualification or certificate of competence. The purpose of the certificate is to impress an employer so that you can get a job. Today, many employers realize that a qualification does not equal the qualities needed for the role on offer. Subsequently, interviews have become longer and more stringent as companies look for additional personal skills and attitudes before taking on an employee. This trend is growing, and academic qualifications are steadily decreasing in significance with major employers. Strategic learners on the other hand view success as the ultimate degree and certificate of competence. Their goal is to succeed and this may involve supplementing their self-directed learning with some formal learning and qualifications, but never involves substituting personal development for formal qualifications.

10. **Learning happens on the exhale:** We inhale information by reading, listening, observing or otherwise taking in new information. However, we exhale it when we explain, share, teach or practice what we have inhaled. True learning occurs as we talk and walk what we have heard and observed. There is no substitute for experience. Learning is accelerated as we dive in and do. This may also mean burning the bridge behind us or removing the safety net beneath us. Strategic learning is not primarily academic in nature; it is practical and must be implemented as part of a real plan to achieve real goals.

I.R.A. (Identify issues, take Responsibility, Action plan)

    1. How has mis-education influenced the person I am today?

_____
_____
_____
_____
_____
_____
_____
_____

    2. What opportunities of re-education, if any, have I forgone?

_____
_____
_____
_____
_____
_____
_____
_____

    3. Beginning today, what can I do differently to re-educate myself?

_____
_____
_____
_____
_____
_____
_____
_____

Any goal is
realistic if
you acquire
the knowledge
and develop
the skills

CHAPTER 12

M.O.R.E. FINANCIAL LITERACY

For most people, having a job and earning a paycheck are the keys to personal financial well-being and independence from the government's social safety net. Yet being able to earn a paycheck is not the same as being able to make informed and wise judgments about what to do with money once it reaches your hands. It is at this point that the financial literacy and competence of individuals are put to the test. According to numerous surveys, most individuals (particularly young ones) fail that test. The consequences are severe.

This failure is manifested in the growing debt and credit difficulties of many people today. Failure to use credit wisely can ruin opportunities and result in future financial distress for an individual.

I learned this the hard way—growing up in a home with a mom who did all she could to support four kids. She worked in the furniture factory all day. Then she came home and fixed hair until people in the neighborhood stopped coming. Even though I grew up watching her make money, there was never an opportunity to see how she managed her money. In es-sence, I grew up illiterate of financial responsibility. However, at the age of sixteen, because I was a standout athlete and knew the owners of two department stores, I was given my first credit card. I had to take a test to get my driver's li-cense, but there was no test on financial literacy in order to receive a credit card.

> I HAD TO TAKE A TEST TO GET MY DRIVER'S LICENSE, BUT THERE WAS NO TEST ON FINANCIAL LITERACY TO RECEIVE A CREDIT CARD.

Today, at the age of forty-two, I believe that improv-ing financial literacy, par-ticularly early in life, will result in informed financial decisions for individuals and households being made over the long term.

I believe the basic reason people (especially young people) should strive to become more financially literate is to help make better informed decisions, and to help them to set and reach their personal financial goals. Whatever the specific goal, the payoff to financial literacy is an improved standard of living, a better community, and a sense of confidence about the future

Looking back over my past twenty five years of poor financial decisions, I believe financial literacy should be taught early. This should include information regarding savings and checking accounts, credit and charge cards, compound interest, and investments/insurance.

Too few people, like myself at sixteen, understand compound interest, investment strategies, risk assessment, insurance and other basics of money management. Most people don't realize the benefits and the costs of credit or the role that home ownership plays in helping to accumulate wealth. The roots of the problem are not hard to find. Most people, like myself, acquire financial knowledge haphazardly by trial and error.

Numerous surveys reveal that most people do not learn any principles of personal finance systematically from their parents while growing up! Instead, they pick up bits and pieces in school, from the media, and through their business deal-ings with financial service providers.

Often the in-formation they acquire is misleading or fraught with errors. A story in New York Times reinforces this mes-sage. A survey found that "adults avoid talking to youngsters about budget-ing, saving and giving to charity in much the same way that they recoil from advising them about sex." Their reason, says the sur-vey, "stems partly from a failure to practice what they preach."

> THE ROOTS OF THE PROBLEM ARE NOT HARD TO FIND. MOST PEOPLE LIKE ME ACQUIRE THEIR FINANCIAL KNOWLEDGE HAPHAZARDLY, BY TRIAL AND ERROR.

One way to eliminate haphazard learning is through the introduction of financial literacy concepts early in the education of every child. The term financial literacy is often confused with or used interchangeably with financial education or financial capability. Financial education is the method used to develop financial literacy. Financial capability is built by participating in financial education and through responsible financial activity.

- Financial knowledge and understanding—making sense of everyday, self-interested financial matters;

- Financial skills and knowledge—applying financial knowledge and understanding to predictable and unpredictable situations;

- Financial responsibility—appreciating the impact of financial decisions on both personal and wider cir-cumstances, understanding rights and responsibili-ties, and knowing sources of advice or guidance.

Lois Vitt (of the Institute for Socio-Financial Studies) defines financial literacy somewhat more comprehensively:

ONE WAY TO ELIMINATE HAPHAZARD LEARNING IS THROUGH THE INTRODUCTION OF FINANCIAL LITERACY CONCEPTS EARLY IN THE EDUCATION OF EVERY CHILD.

"Personal financial literacy is the ability to read, analyze, manage and write about the personal financial conditions that affect material well being. It includes the ability to discern financial choices, discuss money and financial issues without (or despite) discomfort, plan for the future, and respond competently to life events that affect everyday financial decisions, including events in the general economy."

According to the *Washington State Department of Financial Institution:*

- 40% of Americans say they live beyond their means.

- Between 25 million and 56 million adults are unbanked (i.e. not using mainstream, insured financial institutions).

- The average household with debt carries approximately $10,000 to $12,000 in total revolving debt and has nine credit cards.

- 50.8% of college-age adults agree with this statement: "I have experienced repeated, unsuccessful attempts to control, cut back or stop excessive money use."

- In 2005, savings rates dipped to minus 0.5 percent, something that hasn't happened since the Great Depression in 1932 and 1933. A negative savings rate means that Americans spent all their disposable income and dipped into past savings or increased their borrowing.

- Americans shelled out more than $24 billion in credit card fees in 2004, an 18% increase over the previous year.

- 45% of college students are in credit card debt, the average credit card debt being more than $3,000.

- University administrators state that they lose more students to credit card debt than to academic failure.

Financial illiteracy was a problem for me twenty five years ago. It continues to be a growing problem throughout the world today. The recent housing crisis has shown that it can have dangerous consequences. There are a few basic financial tips I'd like to share that I believe anyone can use to easily increase their financial literacy. Many of these tips can help save thousands of dollars over a period of just a few years. They may also aid in avoiding some unnecessary pain that mentally and financially crippled me for years. Let's take a look at what you need to know:

1. Checking accounts must be balanced.

Not taking the time to balance your checkbook every month, may increase your risks for overdrafts. You may find yourself spending more than you would like. Set aside one day a month to completely reconcile and balance your checkbook.

2. Credit card interest rates can cripple you.

How many times have you actually read the interest rate on a credit card appli-cation before sending it in? Many now charge rates that are more than what a loan shark would charge, and this can quickly add up, especially over the long term. If your interest rate is over 12%, (which is still quite high) you may want to consider finding a new card with a better rate and transferring your balances to it. However, in the purest of ad-vice avoid credit cards if you can. Pay cash or use your debit card. They have no long range financial bondage attached to them.

3. Good debt is useful.

Although the word *debt* has a bad connotation, there are forms of good debt that will help grow your monthly income. Bad debt occurs when you spend too much and end up with a bunch of things that will only lose value and never repay you the purchase price.

4. Budgeting is essential.

In the midst of the current credit crunch, it is clear that more people need to learn how to budget. It is not difficult once you get started. Taking a more proactive role in your finances will enable you to see big results. Living by a budget is not restrictive; it just gives some restraint.

5. Emergency funds are lifesavers.

It is a good idea to put at least three months of your salary in a savings account to help protect from those rainy days, layoffs and firings.

The importance of financial literacy in these times cannot be underestimated. One thing these economic times have demonstrated is that there is no substitute for financial literacy when it comes to finances (everything from subprime loans to credit default swaps).

I.R.A. (Identify issues, take Responsibility, Action plan)

1. In what ways has my financial literacy/illiteracy affected me?

_____
_____
_____
_____
_____
_____
_____
_____

2. What have I done to increase my financial literacy?

_____
_____
_____
_____
_____
_____
_____
_____

3. What resources can I use to begin improving my life financially?

_____
_____
_____
_____
_____
_____
_____
_____

CHAPTER 13

M.O.R.E. MONEY

"Money will buy anything except happiness and is a ticket to everywhere except heaven."—Unknown

When you study the scriptures you will discover that there are more than 800 scripture passages addressing money. In fact, Jesus talked more about money in his parables than he did about love. Why? A string is attached between our hearts and our wallets. Our treasure is where our heart is.

According to the Bible, money *"answereth all things"* and *"the love of money is the root of all evil."* God never uses money to corrupt us. However, falling into Satan's trap has corrupted many people, including Christians. When greed, deception, and dishonesty characterize the financial lives of people, they are at odds with God and His plan. This is especially harmful to the church. God never uses money to cause believers worry. When believers are worried, frustrated and upset about money it simply means that God is not in control. God said that wealth without worry is His plan for our lives. He promises to meet the needs of those who trust in Him. In addition, God never uses money to build egos in us. Those who accumulate money for self-esteem selfishly want others to notice them or envy them.

Regardless of your personal feelings and approach to money, it is hard to argue that it is a means to an end. Unless you are able to build your own house, grow your own food, and make your own clothes, money is the vehicle to basic sustenance. Beyond that, we can all agree that money helps us support ministry, take care of our families, and even to travel. Understand without a doubt that money can make your life better and easier. Money is amoral—neither good nor bad. It is active and always doing something. Money is a medium of exchange. We will discuss more later.

Money is just a commodity in economics. This may sound strange, but money is "stuff" just like the "stuff" we buy with it. We use it to receive the value of what we produce by working, selling, or investing. Then that value is transferred to something that we need or want such as food, transportation, clothing, shelter, or pleasure. There is, however, something you need to understand about money. Just "having" money doesn't really mean you have wealth. It is possible to have $2000 in your pocket but owe $2,000 on your credit card bill.

A FEW BASIC MONEY PRINCIPLES

1. **Money, income, and wealth aren't the same.** Money is not about how much you make, it's about how much you keep.

2. **Money is about behavior, not about tools you use to manage it.** It requires the right set of behaviors to make the tools and techniques work you use to manage money.

3. **Money (making it and managing it) is a full-time job.** There's more to money than just sitting down once a month to pay bills. You must be aware of your responsibilities all the time, otherwise all that you strive for is liable to be wrecked in an instant.

FOUR KINDS OF MONEY

Understanding the different types of income aids in understanding money. Below are the four basic types of income. Clearly understanding these different types of income, allows you to make better decisions concerning the way you want to acquire your money. There is no right or wrong; it is all about preference. As you review them, you will be naturally drawn toward the type(s) that appeal to YOU.

Earned income is generally referred to as a wage. It is the direct exchange of time and money. In other words, the trading of time for money. Work eight hours, get paid for eight hours. No Work, No Pay! A hourly job, a sole trader, i.e., a plumber, a doctor, or a lawyer are examples of this. You have to be there in order for the business to function and for you to earn a wage.

Residual income is an income model in which the job only has to be done once, albeit correctly. By doing so financial profits are gained over and over without any further effort on your part. Royalties are a great example of this. A percentage of a previously sold product has a re-occurring income, Royalties can come in many forms. Some examples are insurance, a monthly membership product/ service, property returning a rental income, and weekly or monthly subscriptions. Also, legitimate network marketing/ MLM and affiliate programs have proven to be a great method in building a solid residual income.

Leveraged income is an income that is gained by personal self-effort in conjunction with the combined efforts of others. A team, your down-line (if you are in a network marketing/ MLM business) owning a business and employing others to make sales or conduct services that go toward a bottom line are also examples of this.

J. Paul Getty, once the richest man in the world, said, *"I will rather earn from 1% of 100 people's effort than from 100% of my own effort"*.

GOD NEVER USES MONEY TO CORRUPT US.

The best way to envision this is to imagine yourself being multiplied over and over again. Then imagin eeach one of you making YOU more money. It is ultimately the multiplication of your one effort! This is the power and attraction of leveraged income.

Portfolio income is very similar to residual income. The key difference is that this type of income model requires very little to none of your time to sustain it. Investment and high interest-bearing accounts are the best examples of this type of income.

It is important to be aware of these different models and apply them in your debt free, financially independent plan. This is especially true in today's economy. Ultimately there is no right or wrong in what model you prefer. But by understanding these different types of income, you can make a better decision concerning the way in which you want to make your money and create wealth.

Four Important Functions of money

1) Money as a medium of exchange.
The basic function of money in an economy is to act as a medium of exchange. Money has general acceptability and purchasing power so it can act as a medium of exchange. When money is transacted, purchasing power is transacted from one person to another. In earlier periods we followed a barter system—exchanging goods for goods. But most of the time for such exchange to take place, a situation of mutual wants must occur. Each party in the exchange must have precisely what the other party requires, and in an appropriate quantity and at the time required. The use of money as a common medium of exchange has facilitated exchange greatly.

2) Money as a unit of account.
Money customarily serves as a common unit of account or measure of value in terms of which the values of all goods and services are expressed.

3) Money as a standard of deferred payment.
Money also serves as a standard or unit in terms of which deferred or future payments are stated. This applies to payments of interest, CDs, mutual funds, stocks, cash value life insurance and pensions.

4) Money as a store of value.
Money also serves as a store of value i.e., members of the public can hold their wealth in the form of money. This function is derived from

the use of money as a medium of exchange in a two-fold manner. First, the use of money as a medium of exchange breaks down a single barter transaction into two separate transactions of purchase and sale.

The Importance of Saving and Investing money

If debt represents interest working against you, then saving and investing is interest working for you. What is the importance of saving and investing money? We all have heard that saving extra money each month can be a smart move, but why? Why take to mind these extreme money saving techniques?

There are certainly enough people out there who spend every dime they get, and they seem to be doing fine. I was raised with the mindset to think that if I made $4,000 a month and had $4,000 worth of expenses then I was doing fine. If I got a raise to $4,500 a month than I could afford to take on $500 worth of extra expenses each month. We are conditioned to go out and make as much money as humanly possible, and once we do so to spend it all and enjoy the fruits of our labor. It may sound like a great way to live, but it carries a lot of risk with it.

While the money is rolling in you can afford to do pretty much whatever you choose. But what happens when the money stops? What if you get fired? What if you suddenly have to pay some huge and unexpected expense? If you have no money saved and lose your job, the bills remain. The only alternative then is to start using your credit and rack up debt. This leads to higher bills, and in order to maintain the same life-style you now have to make even more money when you do find another job to compensate for the added debt. This is where the importance of saving comes in.

GOD NEVER USES MONEY TO WORRY US.

If you had $20,000 saved and then lost your job, you would actually be OK. Here you have money to pay your bills and you will not be stressed out. When you save money you are better prepared for emergencies and better equipped to take advantage of opportunities that may come your way.

Saving Extra money

Saving extra money is obviously important. But it can seem like an impossibility if you are already struggling to pay bills. Believe me, I know. For many years I lived with the reality of not "paycheck to paycheck", but "catch up to catch up". At the end of each month I continued to have monthly bills but not enough money.

GOD NEVER USES MONEY TO BUILD EGOS IN US.

I thought it was impossible to save money. However, when my financial mentor introduced me to the concept of paying myself first after I gave God his ten percent things changed. If you find yourself where I was, here are some extreme money saving techniques that can really help you put money aside for a rainy day and/or to pay down your debt.

1. Set a Goal

The first step to saving extra money is to determine how much you actually need to save. Experts agree that you should have at least 6 months of reserve just in case you are out of work. But it can't hurt to be more cautious and save a one year reserve.

2. Make a list

Now that you understand the importance of saving money you will need to determine where your money is going. If you are unsure as to where you are spending your money try this. Make a list of all expenses. Keep a record for one month of what/where you are spending money. Review your record and make decisions as to where you can cut back.

3. Start Young—But If You Are Older Just Start

Saving money when you are young is an important lesson. All good lessons and habits begin early, and saving is a skill that everyone needs. Many people, adults included, do not have a good sense of saving for the long run. Besides being a great way to ensure you have enough money for your old age, saving money when you are young can only help your future.

Monitoring your spending and continuing to save is a good way to accumulate wealth. At a modest interest rate of six percent, your money will double after twelve years. Many teens whom I know spend all their earned money so it never has a chance to grow. Saving money is a major discipline that I drill in my son, Jalen's, life. I constantly remind him that now is a prime time to begin saving. Especially since his mother and I pay for almost everything.

You should have fun with some of your wages if you have a job. But you should also save a portion so that it will grow for you without your having to work. Spending money, not only means the loss of that money, but also the interest that could have accumulated by saving it.

"I WILL RATHER EARN FROM 1% OF 100 PEOPLE'S EFFORT THAN FROM 100% OF MY OWN EFFORT".

The ultimate lesson to be understood regarding money is that its value should never be placed above the value of human beings. Money has grown in its power and productivity. Not because society has accorded it ultimate value, but because it has become an instrument and medium for fulfilling human aspirations and elevating people. Money has served as a symbol of the infinite potential for human accomplishment. As such, it has released enormous energy, creativity, and initiative in society. But the ultimate source of that unlimited creative energy is the individual—not money.

Four Things to Do With Money

SOW 10%	**SAVE** 10%
SPEND 70%	**SCATTER** 10%

I.R.A. (Identify issues, take Responsibility, Action plan)

1. On what source(s) of income do I rest my entire life?

_____
_____
_____
_____
_____
_____
_____
_____

2. What would happen if one or more of those sources was depleted?

_____
_____
_____
_____
_____
_____
_____
_____

3. How can I ensure that my financial state will not be in total jeopardy?

_____
_____
_____
_____
_____
_____
_____
_____

CHAPTER 14
NO M.O.R.E. DEBT

This chapter was written and inspired by my financial mentor,
William V. Thompson, with Fatin H. Horton

God created debt, and everything that He created has a purpose. God's original purpose for debt was to help a neighbor in need without charging interest (see Duet. 15:6-11). However, like most things, it has been perverted to oppress the masses for the benefit of the few.

The perverted purpose of debt is to rob you in eight areas that make up every aspect of your life. If the enemy succeeds in destroying just one of these, your life will be drastically affected. If he destroys or affects all of them, then you are destined for destruction, and no finance company, bank, credit union or wealthy family member can help you. God's grace and mercy will be your only hope of recovery. You Can Be M.O.R.E.

1. Worship

The highest call of any believer is the call to worship. John 4:24 says, *"God is a Spirit: and they that worship Him must worship Him in spirit and in truth."* In order for someone to worship effectively, he must be focused on the Father. Isaiah 26:3 says, *"Thou wilt keep him in perfect peace, whose mind is stayed on Thee: because he trusteth in Thee."* However, debt robs you of your focus on God.

During praise and worship, instead of thinking on the Father, people's minds tend to wander and focus on their past due Visa bill, an overdue phone bill, or a late house payment. Because they have lost focus, they have lost their worship. Additionally, because your mind is not on Him, you lose perfect peace. Though you may have peace for a moment, the enemy comes and steals it because it is not the peace of God. Therefore, it's imperfect.

The success of our life centers around our ability to worship. It is in this intimate time spent with the Father that dreams and goals are birthed. Debt seeks to perform an abortion on your dreams so that they never become a reality. Its method of abortion is to steal your worship. Why? Because worship get you in the presence of God, and Jesus said that without Him, we could do nothing (see Jn. 15:5).

When debt takes your worship it becomes your god because it takes God's glory and transfers it to itself. In Psalm 67:5-7, the psalmist declares that when the people praise God, the earth will yield its increase. When debt attacks our worship life, it poisons the ground that our seed is planted in and destroys the earth's potential to yield its increase. Remember that the thief (debt) comes to steal, kill, and destroy, not just your life, but also your seed of worship.

2. Will

It takes gasoline for a car to get from one point to another. Your will is the gasoline that gets you to the place that God wants you to be. It is the motivational factor that propels you to your destiny. Debt is like a siphoning hose that "sucks" your motivation out until your will is broken and you stop caring about anything (e.g., God, bills, work, appearance, etc.). You lose focus of everything that matters because any additional pressure is magnified.

Debt is like an ancient Chinese torture method, where they would lay a prisoner under dropping water. Though the water would fall only one drop at a time, it always fell in the same place with consistency. This would drive a prisoner crazy and break his will to live. It would drive him to the point where he would rather die than continue in that torture.

That's how debt destroys your will. Though small in the beginning, its attack is relentless and consistent, totally breaking down your will to the point where you stop caring about everything. Dams don't break from one huge blast of water. There is a consistent water pressure before the dam actually breaks, and before the breaking there is a cracking.

Many people reading this book have had their will cracked by debt and are on the verge of having it broken. When debt begins to destroy your will, you say things like, "Let them come and repossess everything; I don't care!" Your attitude becomes one of hopelessness and despair, and like a slave (see Chapter 2), you become broken with no drive to fight. *Your dreams of prosperity turn to nightmares of poverty and you become a master of "just making it."*

3. Witness

Why would sinners get saved if they can't see that salvation making a difference in other Christians' lives? The Bible is clear on the importance of financial organization and stewardship, and it is our job to make the Word flesh, or to make it tangible so sinners can see and long for salvation. Debt destroys our witness because it makes salvation unattractive by giving the appearance that the devil is winning.

If an unsaved person can pay his bills on time, loves his wife, have good family relationships and have abundance in finances, your witness is powerless if you can't at least match his productivity—although you should surpass it. Why? Because you make God look unnecessary. When in debt, creditors see your personal life on profile and determine the potency of the Word by the effect it has on you. Therefore, they can't receive your saying that God will make a difference in their lives when they're wondering when He's going to make a difference in yours.

Many times the "Jesus loves you" on our checks is stamped over by "NSF" by the bank. Which do you think stands out to the sinner? Matthew 5:13 talks about salt losing its savor (taste), therefore making it useless. The taste is the effect salt has on what it touches. Debt comes to rob us of our salt, where we won't have any effect on those with whom we have contact. When you go for a loan, the bank pulls up your credit report, not your contribution statement from church. When the loan officer sees it infested with debt (and late payments), your witness losses power outside of the grace of God. *While we have attacked the devil with our giving his counter punch of debts has sent many Christians reeling.*

Many times Christians try to defeat natural enemies with spiritual warfare. Although there is an element of spiritual warfare that is important to our victory, there are natural issues that need to be dealt with before God will manifest deliverance.

Revelation was practical in Jesus' teaching. It needed to be applied naturally so that people could get deliverance and provision for their situation. Our witness is not empowered by our revelations, but by our testimony (sees Rev. 12:11). *Christians must understand that their credit report is written verification of their integrity.*

What testimony of Christ does your credit report give? When a creditor looks at your credit report, he should be able to tell when you got saved. For example, say that from January 1, 1990, to August 15, 1995, you as an unsaved man or woman always paid your bills late. After you got saved in August, the late payments should stop. From that point on there should be a consistent effort to build a track record of on-time payments that should continue after you are caught up. Eventually the debt should be paid off. *If your payment history chronicled your life, would the date of your salvation be obvious?*

4. Wealth

Debt takes your money! Need we say more? Although wealth is one of the most obvious things that debt wants to take, it is also the hardest loss to stop. Debt steals your wealth from you through finance charges, interest payments, and late penalties.

For example, the majority of a house payment goes to the payment of interest and not to the cost of the house in the early years. On a $ 100,000 loan at 9 percent, the payment would be approximately $ 800 (principal and interest). Of the $ 800, approximately $ 700 of each payment for the first year goes to interest. Debt knows that a lack of money is part of a curse, and it limits the resources that can advance the Kingdom of God (see Hag. 1:4-10 TLB; Mal. 3:9-11).

When your money is gone, you lose your effectiveness because instead of focusing on God, you focus on your lack of money. (See "Worship" earlier in this chapter.) Being broke and in debt causes frustration and keeps you discouraged. When people become discouraged *(dis, "without"; courage, "the conquest of fear")*, they stay in fear of opening their mail, seeing their statements, answering the phone, or negotiating payments of old debts. You are forced to work overtime or to obtain a part-time job to make ends meet.

In Haggai 1, the Bible speaks of putting your money into pockets with holes. This was because the people put their money into their house instead of sowing it into the Kingdom of God. When you're in debt, you do the same thing. Because all your money goes to your debt and your living expenses, you "can't afford" to sow. Thus you work for much but gain little. Consider that you now have two powers working against your money: Interest is eating it away and God is blowing it away. In that situation, you can't afford not to sow.

> THE PERVERTED PURPOSE OF DEBT IS TO ROB YOU IN EIGHT AREAS THAT MAKE UP EVERY ASPECT OF YOUR LIFE.

When cash is short, you feel forced to use more credit cards, which in turn creates more debt. At this point, you have been caught by the debt trap (see Chapter 1). When debt takes your wealth, it limits and sometimes strips you of your ability to provide for your family, which causes low self-esteem. Many men have been robbed of their manhood because of their inability to provide for their family due to the effects of debt. Because of this, our society deals with divided homes, high divorce rates, adultery, massive depression, and even suicide—all because debt has taken our wealth.

5. Weapon

The devil sees what most Christians don't see. When most Christians see a $ 100 bill, all they see is $100. The devil sees the $100 bill as a seed (weapon) that has the ability to produce at least a 30-fold and possibly a 100-fold return—and this scares him! If we are going to declare war on debt, we must have a weapon. The weapon that we have in this battle against debt is our seed. Debt understands that a seed has the ability to reproduce when it is available and is sown.

By giving to God through our local church (see Lk. 6:38), to our pastor (see 1 Cor. 9:7-12; Phil. 4:15-19), to other believers (see Prov. 11:24-25), or to the poor (see Prov. 19:17), we allow our seed to be multiplied. When you use the weapon of your seed your army against debt increases. (One of the definitions of the Hebrew word for "wealth" in the Old Testament is "army" [see Deut. 8:18]). Therefore, debt's strategy is to take your seed by destroying your wealth. (See "Wealth" earlier in this chapter.) If you can't sow your seed, it can't reproduce, which in turn limits the power you have to fight back against your debt.

Your seed is designed by God to advance the Kingdom (see Prov. 10:16 TLB) and to help others (see Deut. 15:6-11). In Second Corinthians 9:10-12, Paul says that doing this "causeth through us thanksgiving to God." When we sow into other people's lives, we cause them to praise God and cause God to move on our behalf. Sowing our seed into those who have less than we do guarantees a return (see Prov. 19:17). Therefore, debt takes our seed to constrict its growth and weaken our attack.

A seed exemplifies God as being a provider. When we sow into other people's lives, we are used by God to express Him in the earth. When we have no seed, God can't use us to express Him in the earth. When we have no seed, God can't use us to express His ability to provide in the earth. *Your money (seed) is your life. You work hours of your life for money; therefore, when you give your money, you give your life.* This shows Christ, who gave His life.

We have the opportunity to give our lives. When debt takes your seed, instead of its being used to destroy the works of the devil by supporting missions or building churches, it is used to support the things of the world and so works against you. That which was to be passed on to the next generation of believers has been passed on to heathens. Instead of empowering our kids, we're impoverishing them. The goal of debt is to render you defenseless so that it might eventually destroy you.

> DEBT SEEKS TO PERFORM AN ABORTION ON YOUR DREAMS SO THAT THEY NEVER BECOME A REALITY.

6. Warfare

In 1 Timothy 6:11-12, Paul tells Timothy to "fight the good fight of faith" and "lay hold on eternal life" because that is what he and every other believer has been called to. In other words, every believer has a right to eternal life, but he or she must fight for it. We have already been promised the victory, so the enemy tries to prevent us from coming to fight.

When we are swamped with debt, we lose our will to "fight" the good fight", and consequently we become defeated. When we are consumed with two and three jobs to make ends meet, we become too busy to fight and are entangled with the affairs of the world (see 2 Timothy 2:4). This causes warfare and intimacy with God to become secondary to paying our bills.

A minister who came to our church once said that the biggest problem in the Church's fulfilling its vision is not the devil, for God has already defeated him. Rather, it's debt. Debt constricts our will to pray, intercede, study our Bible, and do the natural things that prepare us to be used by God.

Remember that the Israelites refused to fight the giants in the wilderness because of their size (see Num. 13:27-33). When they considered how big their problem was, they lost their will to fight. Many times when we look at our debt, it appears so insurmountable that we lose our will to fight and consequently are banished to the wilderness for an extended stay.

WHEN DEBT ATTACKS OUR WORSHIP LIFE, IT POISONS THE GROUND THAT OUR SEED IS PLANTED IN AND DESTROYS THE EARTH'S POTENTIAL TO YIELD ITS INCREASE.

God told the children of Israel to search the land to test whether or not they believed that they could possess it. By their rebellion and delay they were defeated by the enemy. Notice that when they were rebuked, they tried to go and possess the land anyway and were destroyed. Why? They were not backed by the word of the Lord. We have a word that "whatsoever we do will prosper" (see Ps. 1:3); "God shall supply all of our need" (see Phil. 4:19); and "we can do all things through Christ" (see Phil 4:13). However, when we get consumed with cares of the world, that word is choked and becomes ineffective (see Mk. 4:18-19). You are distracted from the real issues of life by continuously worrying and wondering about the future.

Debt's goal is to confuse you in the battle of life so that you can be defeated. Confused people see everything from an erroneous viewpoint. Eventually you begin to war against creditors and your spouse, ignoring the real enemy, the devil. Debt has turned you against yourself and your closet ally (spouse), for it knows that a divided kingdom (house) will eventually fall (see Mt. 13:25).

7. Worth

One of our biggest motivational factors is how we feel about ourselves. The less we feel we're worth, the less we'll invest in

YOUR DREAMS OF PROSPERITY TURN TO NIGHTMARES OF POVERTY AND YOU BECOME A MASTER OF "JUST MAKING IT."

ourselves. When attacked by debt, many times we believe the opposite of what God said about us.

In Deuteronomy 15:6, God tells the Israelites that He will make good on His promise of blessing them after the Abrahamic blessing (see Gen. 12:1-3) and that they will lend to and reign over many nations. Debt wants to choke the Word (see "Warfare" earlier in this chapter) and get you to believe contrary to the promise: "I'll never be blessed; I'm cursed!" Debt makes it seem like God doesn't care about you, for if He did, He wouldn't have allowed this to happen. You feel ashamed, worthless, embarrassed, and confused. You lose faith in yourself and the God in you. Eventually, you see God no differently than you see yourself.

However, we forget that our condition is a result of our decisions. People (especially men and parents) lose their sense of worth when they desire to give their wife and children the basics of life but can't.

Debt eventually affects your family name. Proverbs 22:1 states that the worth of your name is more important than the amount of material possessions you have. When a man has a good name, he has favor with both God and man, which is necessary for success. Though Moses had favor with God, he couldn't get the children of Israel out of Egypt until he got favor with Pharaoh. Favor will get you places where money can't.

Debt looks to destroy your name, and ultimately your favor with man. Banks usually don't favor a man who has more debt than income and is late in paying his bills. Creditors are less lenient with someone who has a poor payment history. Your name has direct impact on your future and helps to determine your worth to others. Regardless of your present situation, however, you're valuable and have worth to God; you're His child

> MANY TIMES THE "JESUS LOVES YOU" ON OUR CHECKS IS STAMPED OVER BY "NSF" BY THE BANK. WHICH DO YOU THINK STANDS OUT TO THE SINNER?

8. Work

Webster's Dictionary defines work as "physical or mental activity undertaken to achieve a purpose involving the expenditure of effort." Everything has a purpose and although debt doesn't destroy your ability to work, it does redirect its purpose from gainful employment to slavery. (See Chapter 1, "Slavery.") Keep in mind the story of David and Goliath and the arrangement made by Goliath beforehand (see 1 Sam. 17:8-9). The outcome of the battle with debt will determined the purpose of work for a nation. And the outcome of your battle with debt will determine the purpose of work for your nation (family). The time that God has called you to spend developing your ministry gift and discovering your purpose is consumed because you are a servant to debt's purpose and are constantly working.

Imagine if you never fulfilled the purpose or work that God has called you to do (because you don't find it). The people whom God had predestined you to reach won't be reached and could potentially be locked in hell for eternity—all because debt robbed you of your time to discover your work here in the earth.

You hold the dollar that makes the difference in whether your church builds their new outreach facility or not, but it goes to debt. The person whom you were supposed to meet at an entrepreneurial convention and later marry, you never meet, and so you have to settle for God's backup plan. And finally, the inheritance that your children would have used to go to college and start a business empire and dynasty, they never receive—all because of debt. Debt affects far more than just you; it affects people and generations to come. It robs God's providence of its potency and leaves you wandering instead of achieving.

> INTEREST IS EATING IT AWAY AND GOD IS BLOWING IT AWAY.

To be a servant to the purpose of debt makes you an enemy to the purpose of God (see Mt. 12:30). God can't trust His enemies with the keys to the Kingdom (see Mt. 16:13-21); therefore, the wealth that is laid up for you becomes unattainable (see Prov. 13:22). When you're overloaded with debt, the desire for ministry is gone because all your energy is exhausted by fighting debt. Remember that debt is only one of many tactics used by the devil, and if all your energy is exerted in fighting debt and trying to meet your needs, how can you meet the needs of others?

I.R.A. (Identify issues, take Responsibility, Action plan)

1. Make a list of current debt.

_____
_____
_____
_____
_____
_____
_____
_____

2. How/why did I incur these debts?

_____
_____
_____
_____
_____
_____
_____
_____

3. What can I do to begin eliminating these debts and prevent future debt?

_____
_____
_____
_____
_____
_____
_____

Money has grown in its power and productivity not because society has accorded it ultimate value, but because it has become an instrument and medium for fulfilling human aspirations and elevating people.

CHAPTER 15

M.O.R.E. MENTORS

"We learn wisdom two ways, the mistakes of our mentors or the mistakes of one self."—Anthony Q. Knotts

L ife has given us two very powerful teachers. Each is a first class instructor, but neither come without a price. While both are effective, both demand something of us.

The teachers are Mentors and Mistakes. While we can learn great lessons from either teacher, we have to choose one or the other. If we choose neither, the second will be chosen for us. Take note, however, of the very different teaching styles of each. While your Mentor will be excited and delight you with his or her wisdom, Mistakes will leave you breathless—and not in a positive way. The truth is, the latter is by far the tougher teacher of the two.

Mistakes' down payments as well as its ongoing payments are very expensive. Believe me, while Mistakes teaches you well, by the time her lessons are learned, her instruction may have cost you years. It may have cost our marriages, our families, our careers, our ministries, and perhaps even our lives.

While growing up in the projects, there were always older guys whom I looked up to and followed around. One day I decided to hang out with the boys. The end was major trouble. The decision to burn cat-o-ninetails in the sewage system resulting in setting the entire system afire. The fire department came and, as God would have it, we were seen as we made our getaway. Man, did I think my mom's whipping would literally kill me! I couldn't sit down for a week.

Needless to say, my days of hanging out with those boys were over. Each of us has learned something from personal experience that has made us a little wiser. But such lessons—lessons learned from mistakes—inflict real suffering and serious pain. Sometimes they're much more harmful than setting sewage on fire.

If Mistakes has a back end price then Mentors has a front end price. Mentors requires patience, consistency, and above all, time. Do you want to know the biggest difference between Mistakes and Mentors? Mentors teach the lesson before you make the mistake. While Mistakes demand that you bump your head before you learn the lesson.

What is mentoring?

Mentoring is a developmental partnership. One person shares experiences (good or bad), skills, mistakes, wisdom, and perspective to foster the spiritual, personal, professional or financial growth of someone else. This sharing is based on trust, truth and transparency on the part of both parties.

We all have a need for insight that is outside of our normal life and educational experience. The power of mentoring is that it creates a one-of-a-kind opportunity for collaboration, goal achievement, and problem solving. We can only go so far by ourselves. One of my favorite sayings is "Left to yourself, you will self destruct." We all need mentors!

Types of mentoring

- Informal—This is the type most people think of when they hear of mentoring. It is a spontaneous, casual relationship in which a trained person takes an untrained person "under his or her wing" and provides guidance and counsel. Many people who want this type of mentoring do not receive it. The desire to allow everyone access to mentoring has led many organizations to start "formal" or structured mentoring programs.

- Structured—This type of mentoring is designed to create a culture in which people can proactively support the development of one another. In these programs, mentors are generally matched with mentees to support specific goals such as leadership development, diversity, or retention.

Mentoring can be delivered:

- One-on-one, typically with a more trained person mentoring an untrained individual.

- In teams consisting of peers with different backgrounds and skills, mentoring each other or a small group matched with a more seasoned person. Peer mentoring teams are effective since they are based on the concept of mutual benefit. Participants receive support and advice as they provide support and advice for others.

The Differences Between Coaching & mentoring

Mentoring and coaching are often seen as similar or even the same. However, as you will see, they are not. My experience with mentors began after the bad decision of purchasing a sports car in my sophomore year of college led to my dropping out. I had been playing sports since I was eight years old. Throughout this time my experiences had been with coaches. But a bad decision led to the beginning of wonderful experiences with mentors in many different areas of my life. I found that there are three important differentiators between mentoring and coaching.

Differentiator #1:

Coaching is task oriented. The focus is on concrete issues, such as effective management, articulation of speech, and strategic thinking. These are tasks which require a content expert (coach) capable of teaching the development of these skills.

Mentoring is relationship oriented. It seeks to provide a safe environment for the mentee to share issues which affect his or her spiritual, professional and personal success. Although specific learning goals or competencies may be used as a basis for creating the relationship, its focus goes beyond these areas. It may include work/life balance, selfconfidence, self-perception, and how the personal influences the professional.

Differentiator #2:

Coaching is short term. A coach can successfully be involved with a student for a short period of time—maybe even just a few sessions. The coaching lasts for as long as is needed, depending on the purpose of the coaching relationship.

Mentoring is always long term. Successful mentoring requires time. Both partners learn about one another and build a climate of trust where the mentee can feel secure in sharing the real issues that impact his or her success. Successful mentoring relationships last nine months to a lifetime.

Differentiator #3:

Coaching is performance driven. The purpose of coaching is to improve the individual's performance at hand. This involves either enhancing current skills or acquiring new skills. Once the student successfully acquires the skills, the coach is no longer needed.

Mentoring is development driven. Its purpose is to develop the mentee not only for the present, but also for the future. This requires an ongoing relationship between the mentor and the mentee because the aim is continued growth, not simply an immediate goal.

Mentoring Examples in the Bible

Although the Bible doesn't use the words mentor, mentee, or mentoring, it frequently refers to what we believe are successful mentoring relationships: Jesus and His disciples, Barnabas and Paul, Paul and Timothy, Naomi and Ruth, Elijah and Elisha, Moses and Joshua, Deborah and Barak, Elizabeth and Mary (the mother of Jesus), and many others. All are powerful examples of pairs and the God-inspired actions they took to help each other develop.

Moses and Joshua (Mentor and Mentee) aptly illustrate a successful mentoring partnership. Moses demonstrated the wisdom of a mentor by deciding to delegate an important task (Exodus 17:9). He placed one of his soldiers, Joshua, in command of a battle with the Amalekites over a water dispute. In making this decision, Moses demonstrated trust in Joshua's gifts and leadership potential. He opened the way for their ongoing teamwork. This is the first time this "mentor" asked someone else to lead an attack, one of many that his "mentee" Joshua would command. Did they sit down and negotiate this developmental relationship, calling each other mentor and mentee? Probably not. It's more likely that Moses wasn't aware of applying mentoring principles and didn't necessarily regard Joshua as his mentee. Yet the ingredients of mentoring were there, and Joshua entered a relationship with a respected man that changed Joshua's life forever.

Following this successful assignment, Joshua became a frequent companion of Moses. Even though he was called a servant (Exodus 24:13, 33:11), he was actually more of a colleague. (Notice in Exodus 3:11, Joshua refused to leave with Moses, something that would not have been permitted of a servant.) Their mentoring relationship deepened, and Joshua gained valuable knowledge, skills, and confidence. We find evidence that their mutual trust increased when

LIFE HAS GIVEN US TWO VERY POWERFUL TEACHERS. EACH IS A FIRST CLASS INSTRUCTOR, BUT NEITHER COME WITHOUT A PRICE.

Moses allowed his mentee to accompany him to an important meeting with none other than God (Exodus 24:13-14)! We're not sure that Joshua was actually with Moses in the presence of the Lord, but we know for certain that he was on the mountain (Exodus 32:17) and talked with Moses on their return to the camp. Imagine the incredible lessons Joshua received that day!

Moses took Joshua to another meeting in a special tent where Moses spoke with God again. Joshua chose to stay at the tent after Moses left to return to camp (Exodus 33:11), where he remained on his own in the presence of God. Moses demonstrated significant trust by not interfering in this major opportunity for Joshua.

MISTAKES TEACHES YOU WELL, BUT BY THE TIME WE LEARN HER LESSONS, HER INSTRUCTION MAY HAVE COST US YEARS.

Moses continued to offer Joshua opportunities to develop. He assigned him (along with 11 other men) to seek out the Promised Land. The mentor gave him a job that required a plan, teamwork, and a report (Numbers 13:16). Moses probably also provided some suggestions for how to carry out this plan.

Finally, Moses affirmed his mentee by commissioning Joshua in the presence of the people of Israel (Deuteronomy 31:7-8). He gave Joshua public recognition for the lessons he learned. What's more, Moses conferred power on his mentee, and vacated his position to him. Their formal mentoring relationship ended. When Moses died, Joshua was appointed as the new leader of Israel and later took his people into the Promised Land (Numbers 27:15-23). Moses provided a great lesson in how to transfer leadership. A time comes to either step aside to allow our successors to lead in our place or allow them to move on to a place of leadership elsewhere. Moses gave the proper direction, teaching, and recognition to prepare Joshua to fulfill his role in life.

The mentoring relationship of Moses and Joshua was very task-and-performance oriented. They provide clear-cut illustrations of several excellent mentor activities:

- *assigning* the mentee preliminary stretch tasks

- depending on the mentee's initial performance, making *additional assignments* requiring more skills and responsibilities

- *inviting* him (or her) to *key events*

- allowing the mentee to *observe the mentor* in action

- *affirming* the mentee for achievements

- *stepping aside* to let the mentee succeed

Main Issues Related to Mentoring

For the mentoring process to be most effective, certain issues and barriers must be predicted—with proper expectations set in advance. First, both parties must be willing to enter the relationship with an agreement that coercion will never be used. To avoid coercion, it is essential to consider the differences between assessment and evaluation. Mentors and mentees vary widely in personality styles, purposes, and assumptions about how to achieve improvements in performance and growth.

The relationship between the individuals must have clear boundaries that are identified through careful discussion between the parties. In many cases, mentees have significant life barriers that influence the success of the mentoring process and relationship. The module provides assessment suggestions and resources (such as work on a life vision portfolio or referral to a mental health professional) for working with preliminary barriers to growth. Because it is not possible to predict how a mentor/mentee relationship will evolve, mentors must facilitate an appropriate level of challenge and mentees must accept the challenge with honesty and openness, especially when things are not going as well as hoped.

Mentoring (whether spiritual, personal, or professional) is an important strategy for enhancing specific areas of growth that are not yet required, but that are likely to support future success in a mentee's life. It is clear that the valuable insights gained during mentoring will substantially improve transfer of learning both for the mentor and the mentee. Mentors benefit from servant-leadership experiences that can add meaning and purpose to their lives as experienced professionals. For mentees, the process opens a window on their futures and on themselves, by making it possible to experience growth that may not have happened had they been left to their own devices. Mentoring is an essential process, especially in the fast changing world of higher education.

MENTORING
(WHETHER SPIRITUAL,
PERSONAL, OR PROFESSIONAL)
IS AN IMPORTANT
STRATEGY FOR
ENHANCING
SPECIFIC AREAS OF
GROWTH THAT ARE
NOT YET REQUIRED,
BUT THAT ARE LIKELY
TO SUPPORT
FUTURE SUCCESS IN
A MENTEE'S LIFE.

I.R.A. (Identify issues, take Responsibility, Action plan)

1. In what areas do I need a mentor the most?

    _____
    _____
    _____
    _____
    _____
    _____
    _____
    _____

2. What mistakes have I made as a result of lacking guidance (mentorship)?

    _____
    _____
    _____
    _____
    _____
    _____
    _____
    _____

3. Who would I like to be my mentor? Why?

    _____
    _____
    _____
    _____
    _____
    _____
    _____
    _____

CHAPTER 16

NO M.O.R.E. EXCUSES

"Winners make goals, losers make excuses."—Unknown

R ecently CNBC Titans aired a documentary on Ted Turner, the owner of the Atlanta Braves. I grew up an avid Braves fan. In fact, my first trip outside of Lexington, Joel Stutts (from the Parks and Recreation) took us to a game in Atlanta. Being only eight years of age at the time, I didn't have a really good grasp of what Ted Turner, the team owner, had accomplished both personally and professionally. Thirty four years later I now realize that Mr. Turner epitomizes the word entrepreneur, risk-taker and one who accomplished all he did without making excus-es. He is not only the owner of the World Series winning Atlanta Braves but the founder of TBS and CNN, as well as, America's Cup sailing champion. In addition to all of this, he is one of the world's biggest philanthropists.

No matter what the endeavor Ted never made excuses as to why he couldn't do it. Everyone in life goes through ups and downs, and yet the majority of people don't cel-ebrate the ups—and complain about the downs. Ted's sis-ter passed away from cancer at the age of seventeen, his parents separated, and then his father committed suicide by shooting himself. All of this occurred prior to Ted turn-ing twenty-four years of age. Does this sound like a regu-lar upbringing? For most of us, probably not.

> AN EXCUSE IS SOMETHING WE MAKE TO CONVINCE OURSELVES THAT THE TASK IS NOT WORTH DOING.

Even though Ted was left with his father's one million dollar billboard business under his control, he was a twenty-four year old Brown University dropout. He had experience in working for the business, not running it. He had been through major personal turmoil yet we know how the story ends. Ted is one of the world's greatest billionaires and philanthropists. How can this happen?

This chapter is not just about Mr. Turner and his path to success. It's about the principles behind making excuses and why we limit our success. His story is just a perfect ex-ample to follow. In fact, many people, including Oprah, Martha Stewart, Jay Z, and Steve Jobs all went through personal hardships. All of these people were given many reasons why they should give up, yet didn't. They have managed to overcome them and succeed.

An excuse is something made up to convince ourselves that the task is not worth doing. Don't feel like going to the gym this morning? It is raining and cold, after all. Don't feel like going to church? I can watch it on TV. Like these two examples, most excuses are small and appear harmless. But excuses limit us from living our lives to the fullest. This is where the problems begin. In life, ministry, and entrepreneurship, there are a million reasons to just give up and become a typical person and get a job. Things take four times longer than they should, you have no money, people don't believe in you, your family thinks you are crazy, etc. There are plenty of reasons to just stop what you are doing.

Ted Turner had every opportunity, every reason to just give up ownership of his father's company, take a working role and live a decent life. He could have wallowed in the sadness of the tragedies in his life and turned to drugs and alcohol to heal his pain. One of the most common ex-cuses for becoming drug addicts and alcoholics is "my parents got divorced when I was young".

> REMEMBER, THE WORLD IS FILLED WITH EXCUSES WHY YOU SHOULDN'T DO SOMETHING.

Ted, instead, within a few years, grew his father's company into a much larger version. This alone is something that can take a lifetime to do. He then decided that he wanted to have more of a global impact. To him, making sales on billboards had very little impact on the world. So he decided to buy a small television station in Atlanta. At that time, the only national TV stations were NBC, CBS and ABC. All the others were just local stations, having to struggle to get any kind of distribution. In Atlanta, the station was boring and losing money. Because things had always been done a certain way, this was yet another opportunity for Ted to just stop what he was doing and go back to the "safe" advertising business. Instead, he thought that putting the Atlanta Braves on his station would increase ratings. Not only did ratings explode, but when the Braves came up for sale, Mr. Turner thought it would be a good idea to purchase them.

Many people, including family members, thought he was crazy. Ted was able to push aside any excuses the people around him offered and just go out and do what he thought was best.

> WHEN YOU DECIDE TO STOP MAKING EXCUSES AND INSTEAD MAKE PROGRESS, YOUR WHOLE WORLD CHANGES.

He made some great decisions and a couple of very poor ones. At one point during the AOL—Time Warner merger, he was losing $10 million in stock value per day. He was once worth $10 billion, and it collapsed to $1.9 billion. Instead of complaining and going into hiding, Ted opened up forty-eight restaurants serving premier bison beef.

Many of us operate on much, much smaller numbers. We live our lives for the most part follow-ing other people's paths. We often do not stop to think whether what we are doing is right for us. We al-low other people to make excuses for us as to why or why not to do something. The worst part—we listen. Instead of putting on blinders and doing what our gut tells us to do, we listen to others who speak from their past experiences.

When it comes to careers, you have the choice of deciding to go into what you know is right for you or listen-ing to other people as to why it won't work. You can use past downfalls as excuses for why you won't succeed, or you can put your head down and create a future. You can blame your parents for not raising you properly and giv-ing you the wealth you "deserve", or you can thank them for instilling a sense of drive and an appreciation of mon-ey. Remember, the world is filled with excuses as to why you shouldn't do something. The question is, are you go-ing to let those excuses creep into your mind and keep you from being, doing and having more?

EXCUSES ARE A PREREQUISITE FOR QUITTING.

Brian Tracey said "When you decide to stop making excuses and instead make progress, your whole world changes. When you discipline yourself to take action rather than to procrastinate, you feel a surge of self-esteem, self-respect and personal power. You put yourself in control of your life and your destiny."

Many people have the disease "excuse-itis," the habit of making excuses for problems and difficulties in life. But all high-achievers, leaders, and exceptional men and women refuse to make excuses. Instead, they accept responsibil-ity and take action to overcome their obstacles and move forward.

Excuses are a prerequisite for quitting. If you justify your reasons for failing enough, it's easy to quit and just blame it on the issues you encountered. This has aided me in creating a list which I believe reflects the top 5 excuses people use to sabotage their lives. I'm going to share it with you.

1. People Can't Really Change

If this is your starting point, you're in trouble. I believe that many people sabotage their lives simply because they don't really believe they or any other human being, for that matter, can consciously change. They buy too much into that theory that a leopard cannot change its spots.

While I think there are limits to how much and how fast we can change, the rest is complete nonsense. The fact that some people don't really change after the age of fifteen doesn't mean that people in general can't change. It rather means that many people don't really understand the psychology of change or how to undergo effective change.

> EXCUSES WILL PREVENT YOU FROM REACHING YOUR FULL POTENTIAL AND TO SUCCEED IN LIFE.

2. My Situation Is Special

I, for one, find this excuse amusing. We are so arrogant as to believe the rules that apply for every other person do not apply for us. When I present a client a tried and tested method to communi-cate better with others, they will often admit that it may work for others, but assume it won't work for them.

I'll state it plain and simple here: you are not special! If something works for 99% of the people who've applied it, it's highly probable it will work for you as well. Let your guard down and try it before you declare that it doesn't apply in your context.

3. I Had a Bad Childhood

This is something I can understand. However, the amount of emphasis people tend to put on their past, even ending up believing that it's an in surmountable obstacle is foreign to me. They often use a bad childhood as an excuse for having a bad life and without doing anything to try to negate it.

One of the most important discoveries in cognitive psychology is that even though many of our thinking, feeling and behavior patterns have been created in the past, sometimes in our childhood they have a life of their own in the here and now.

It is in the here and now that we can act upon them and we can influence them.

4. I'm Too Old/ Too Young

There's a whole range of utilized excuses related to sex, race, nationality and age. The ones related to age, I find to be the most devious.

At one time, I thought my young age was preventing people from trusting me as a pastor. This in turn was preventing me from enlisting more mature members. Fortunately, I soon realized that although some people did have a bias against young coaches, it was mostly in my head. As soon as I stopped treating my young age as a drawback, so did other people.

> EXCUSES MAKE YOU WANT PEOPLE TO LOOK AT YOU AS "POOR YOU"—A VICTIM OF OTHER PEOPLE'S MISTAKES.

There are certainly age prejudices, and your age can present a challenge. However, keep in mind that age is a surmountable obstacle and we can maneuver around it. This is why, in my view, it provides a really superficial excuse for not doing or not getting something.

5. I Will Start Tomorrow

Sure! And following that same logic, tomorrow you will see no reason why you can't say the exact same thing. After all, what's a day plus or minus, right? Do this long enough and you eventually realize that you've postponed things so long they don't seem worth doing anymore.

Take a deep breath and take a good look at the five excuses above. Have you been using any of them lately? Can you see how they sabotage you much more than they support you? Living an extraordinary life, having an extraordinary career or extraordinary relationships, these things do not happen by making excuses. Excuses will prevent you from reaching your full potential and succeeding in life. If you make excuses every time you fail or someone around you fails it will end up being a belief, which becomes a self-fulfilling prophecy. Charles C. Noble once said, "First we make our habits, then our habits make us."

Excuses hinder and stop you from progressing. They make you focus on pleasing people and how people should perceive you as a winner when you are not. Excuses make you want people to look at you as "POOR YOU"—a victim of other people's mistakes. This halts your progress. Oprah Winfrey said it better: "I don't think of myself as a poor deprived ghetto girl who made good. I think of myself as somebody who from an early age knew I was responsible for myself, and I had to make good."

The problem is—with time, people will know your song without you realizing it. They will just say, "here we go again; excuses, excuses in their hearts". They will avoid you and won't want to hang around you. Nobody wants to engage in business with people that make excuses! To be honest, people that assume responsibility are the ones who gain respect and trust from people around them. People know those that assume responsibility for their shortcomings are 98% likely to seek a solution and take action to make things better.

Your success and failure depends on you. It is based on the decisions you make. So you need to cultivate an attitude that accepts responsibility for failure and success.

The time has dawned upon you to stop making excuses. Stop creating excuses, but begin creating solutions and ways to improve life. Please know and believe that God created you to be, do and have MORE. Today is a new day, you're now beginning to head in a new direction. You can turn excuses into execution.

Please know that Byrdie and I believe that YOU CAN BE MORE!

I.R.A. (Identify issues, take Responsibility, Action plan)

1. What do I most often make excuses about in my life?

    _____
    _____
    _____
    _____
    _____
    _____
    _____
    _____
    _____

2. Why do I make excuses instead of accepting responsibility?

    _____
    _____
    _____
    _____
    _____
    _____
    _____
    _____
    _____

3. How can I practice taking ownership of my actions?

    _____
    _____
    _____
    _____
    _____
    _____
    _____
    _____
    _____

ABOUT THE AUTHOR
Anthony Q. Knotts

Anthony Q. Knotts is an enterprising entrepreneur with a passion to impact the world through biblical and business principles. He has acquired substantial wisdom from his experience as a businessman in the technology market, an international conference orator, and founding pastor of The Embassy Church International in Greensboro, NC. He is the president of Manna Enterprises, Inc., a video and mobile marketing company, and M.O.R.E., Inc., a movement designed to Motivate Others to Reach Excellence. His influence extends to a diversity of audiences, spanning from elementary to high school and from college to corporate. Anthony is also an official ambassador for Joseph's House, Inc., a nonprofit organization dedicated to improving the lives of homeless young men in Guilford County, NC. Additionally, he is a certified iCAN (International Coaching Achievers Network) coach in partnership with Wayne Malcolm of London, England.

Anthony and his wife, Byrdzetta, have three children: Teland, Jalen and Destiny.